Diana Goodey   Noel Goodey

Messages

Student's Book

2

CAMBRIDGE
UNIVERSITY PRESS

	Grammar	Vocabulary and Pronunciation	Listening and Reading skills	Communicative tasks
Module 1 My life — **Unit 1** Getting started	• Revision: *be, there is/are, can, have got, live ...* • *Like + -ing* • Revision: Question forms	• Expressing opinions • Revision: adjectives • Interests and activities	• Read a variety of short texts • Listen to different opinions • Read about a British teenager • *Story: Wild Flowers* 1 • *Life and culture:* I live in New York	• Write about your class • Exchange opinions • Write the results of an opinion poll • Talk about your interests • Ask for and give personal information
Unit 2 A slice of life	• Present simple: affirmative, negative, questions • Frequency adverbs	• Expressions of frequency • Everyday routines • Link words • /s/ /z/ and /ɪz/	• Read about teenagers in the USA • Read about everyday routines • Listen to a song • *Story: Wild Flowers* 2 • *Life and culture:* Making music	• Write about life in your country • Talk about your routines • Do a questionnaire • Write about your average day
Review	*Study skills:* Using your book *How's it going?:* Progress check *Coursework:* Life in Britain

Module 2 In the past — **Unit 3** Stories	• Past simple of *be* • Past simple of regular and irregular verbs: affirmative, negative	• Numbers and dates • Holidays • Pronunciation: *13, 30, 30th*	• Listen and find the right picture • Read a text and guess the missing words • Read a poem • *Story: Wild Flowers* 3 • *Life and culture:* The garden-chair pilot	• Invent and talk about 'a world record' • Write about a holiday • Discuss and write a short story
Unit 4 Entertainment	• Past simple: questions and short answers • Questions with *What, Which, How,* etc.	• Jobs • Past time expressions • /t/ /d/ and /ɪd/	• Listen and answer personal questions • Read and order a story • Listen to a song • *Story: Wild Flowers* 4 • *Life and culture:* Making movies	• Write and ask questions for a quiz • Talk about an amazing weekend • Write and act an interview with a star • Write about a visit to the cinema
Review	*Study skills:* Punctuation *How's it going?:* Progress check *Coursework:* Biographies

Module 3 Out and about — **Unit 5** On the move	• Present continuous: affirmative, negative, questions • Present continuous and present simple	• In town • Directions • Stress in words	• Read a notice and a newspaper article • Listen to directions and follow on a map • Read and listen to a rap • Listen to short conversations at a station • *Story: Wild Flowers* 5 • *Life and culture:* The Eco-Challenge Race	• Ask for and give directions • Talk about what you're doing at the moment • Write and act a telephone conversation • Write about an imaginary person
Unit 6 Echoes of the past	• *There was / It was* • Past continuous: affirmative, negative, questions • *could/couldn't*	• Places • Intonation in questions	• Read a short history text • Listen to and identify sounds • *Story: Wild Flowers* 6 • *Life and culture:* The first Americans	• Talk about life in the past • Talk and write about your town in the past • Describe what was happening at a particular time • Write a ghost story • Talk about things someone could and couldn't do
Review	*Study skills:* Remembering vocabulary *How's it going?:* Progress check *Coursework:* A weekend in Manchester

		Grammar	Vocabulary and Pronunciation	Listening and Reading skills	Communicative tasks
Module 4 It's different!	**Unit 7** Differences	• Comparatives: -er/more ... than • as ... as • Possessive pronouns • Whose ... ?	• Adjectives • Computers • Modern inventions • Rhythm drill: /ə/	• Listen to a telephone conversation • Read a newspaper article • Story: Swim! 1 • Life and culture: Poem – Mum, Dad and Me	• Write an advert and compare things • Talk about differences and similarities • Talk about people's possessions
	Unit 8 Our incredible world	• Superlatives • The future with going to: affirmative, negative, questions • The comparative and superlative of good and bad	• How + adjective + is it? • /ɪ/ and /iː/	• Listen to and complete a conversation • Read a school essay • Story: Swim! 2 • Life and culture: The longest road in the world	• Talk about famous places and things • Ask questions about your country or town • Talk about your plans • Describe plans for a trip • Share your opinions
	Review	*Study skills:* Recognising sentence patterns *How's it going?:* Progress check *Coursework:* Superlative places!			
Module 5 A healthy future	**Unit 9** Looking ahead	• The future with will: affirmative, negative, questions • Present continuous used for the future	• Important events • Future time expressions • /w/	• Read a magazine article • Listen to a song • Story: Swim! 3 • Life and culture: A basketball star	• Write predictions about a friend • Ask and answer questions about events in the future • Talk about future arrangements • Practise a telephone conversation
	Unit 10 Some ketchup, please!	• Countable and uncountable nouns • Polite requests and offers: I'd like ... , Could I have ... , Would you like ... ? • How much/many? • a lot of / much / many	• Food and drink • Weak forms	• Listen for food vocabulary • Read about an average person in the USA • Story: Swim! 4 • Life and culture: Would you like some waffles?	• Ask for and offer food and drink • Write and act a conversation in a canteen • Make questions for a 'quantity' quiz • Write about your lifestyle
	Review	*Study skills:* Guessing what words mean *How's it going?:* Progress check *Coursework:* On holiday			
Module 6 Our world	**Unit 11** In the wild	• Can/can't for possibility • Must/mustn't for obligation • Should/shouldn't for advice	• Verbs of action • /ʊ/ and /uː/	• Read notices • Listen to a radio programme • Read a book review • Story: Swim! 5 • Life and culture: A letter from Canada	• Talk and write about rules at your school • Write a letter asking for advice • Give advice • Share your opinions about what people should and shouldn't do
	Unit 12 Who cares?	• Revision: expressing opinions, must, should • First conditional	• Everyday materials • /æ/ and /e/	• Read about the environment • Listen to an argument between a teenager and her parents • Read about the tiger • Listen to a song • Story: Swim! 6 • Life and culture: The World Wide Fund For Nature	• Talk about a survey • Talk and write about recycling and the environment • Make a poster
	Review	*Study skills:* Studying at home *How's it going?:* Progress check *Coursework:* A visit to my country			

• Grammar index • Communicative functions index • Wordlist • Irregular verbs • Spelling notes • Phonetic symbols • Songs

Module 1

My Life

In Module 1 you study

Grammar

- *Be, can, have got, there is/are*
- Question forms
- *Like + -ing*
- Present simple
- Frequency adverbs

Vocabulary

- Expressing opinions
- Adjectives
- Interests and activities
- Expressions of frequency
- Everyday routines
- Link words

so that you can

- Talk about facts
- Write some facts about your class
- Understand, ask for and express opinions
- Talk about things you like and don't like
- Ask for and give personal information
- Talk about your daily life
- Describe what other people do
- Talk about how often you do things
- Write a questionnaire about your favourite pastimes
- Talk about everyday routines
- Write about your average day

Wild Flowers

Chapter 1 – Where's Mr Roberts?
Chapter 2 – Tom wants to find out

Life and culture

I live in New York
Making Music

Coursework 1

Life in Britain
You write a newsletter about your country.

Life in Britain

Hi! In my first newsletter, I'm going to tell you a bit about life in Britain.

There are three countries in Britain – England, Scotland and Wales – and there are 58 million people. The people are a mixture of different nationalities and ethnic groups. For example, 2.3 million people are Asian.

In Britain school starts about nine o clock and finishes about three thirty. People usually start work between eight and nine and finish between five and six.

A lot of my friends do sport in their free time. The British are great sports fans.

What's it about?

What can you say about the pictures?

Now match the pictures with sentences 1–4.

1 I think it's great.
2 Teenagers in the USA like rollerblading.
3 He works in the Antarctic.
4 The alarm clock rings at half past seven.

Coursework
My window on the world

In Book 2 you study
● the language of the world around you

so that you can
● describe life in your country, and complete an English Coursework folder

Your Coursework has got six parts:

Part 1 Life in Britain
You write a newsletter about your country.

Part 2 Biographies
You write about famous people in your country.

Part 3 A weekend in Manchester
You write about your town, or your capital city.

Part 4 Superlative places!
You draw a map of your country and write about places there.

Part 5 On holiday
You write about holidays in your country.

Part 6 A visit to my country
You write about a visit to your country.

1 Getting started

In Step 1 you study
- *be, there is/are, can, have got, live, eat,* etc.

so that you can
- talk about facts
- write some facts about your class

1 Reading *What do you know?*

a ⏱ Read the texts. Find at least three words you don't understand. Look in your dictionary or ask your teacher. You've got four minutes!

b Match the words in A with the words in B. Make ten true sentences.

1 *Little Italy isn't in Italy.*

A	B
1 Little Italy	a can understand sign language.
2 People in Britain	b you can hear Spanish, Italian and Chinese.
3 There	c isn't in Italy.
4 Owls	d can't fly.
5 The red-kneed tarantula	e drink a lot of tea.
6 Penguins	f hasn't got a mobile phone.
7 'General Sherman'	g are cheetahs in Africa and Asia.
8 In New York	h lives in Mexico.
9 Matt Long	i have got powerful eyes.
10 Chimpanzees	j is a very tall tree.

2 Grammar revision *Verbs*

Complete the sentences with these words.

is   are   There's   There are   can   can't
has got   have got   haven't got   eat   lives

1 Owls _can_ see very well at night.
2 People in the USA _____ seven million pizzas every day.
3 Penguins _____ wings but they _____ fly.
4 _____ a place called El Barrio in New York.
5 Spiders _____ six legs.
6 'General Sherman' _____ 83 metres tall.
7 Chimpanzees _____ very intelligent animals.
8 _____ 290 million people in the USA.
9 The red-kneed tarantula _____ red knees. It _____ in a hole in the ground.

THE WORLD OF ANIMALS

The cheetah lives in Africa and Asia. It has got very powerful legs. It can run 100 kilometres an hour.

Penguins can swim but they can't fly.

Chimpanzees can't talk but they can use sign language.

Owls have got very large eyes. They can see in the dark.

MANCHESTER EVENING GAZETTE

Letters to the editor

I want to start an 'Anti-Mobiles' group. I think mobile phones are dangerous and I don't think they are necessary. If you agree, please write to me.

Matt Long
231 Albert Terrace
Manchester MN4 9FZ
mattdlong@yourline.co.uk

Visit the Big Apple

New York is an exciting and beautiful city. People of many different nationalities live here. Little Italy, El Barrio and Chinatown are all parts of New York.

There's a spider in Mexico with red knees. It's called the Mexican red-kneed tarantula.

There's a tree in California called General Sherman. It's 83 metres tall.

There are 60 million people in Britain.
The British drink 185 million cups of tea every day.

3 Reading and speaking
Facts and opinions

a Which of these sentences is a fact? Which sentence is an opinion?

1 Penguins can't fly.
2 I think mobile phones are dangerous.

Find a fact in the texts that you think is interesting. Read it to the class and give your opinion.

> Owls can see in the dark. I think that's interesting.

b Can you complete these sentences?

1 The capital of *Brazil* is *Brasilia* .
2 There are .... people in our country.
3 We eat a lot of ....
4 Bats can't ....
5 Chicago is ....

c If you have time, think of more facts and tell the class.

4 Speaking and writing *Facts about us*

Use what you know

Make sentences about your class.

There are thirty people in our class.
My friend Jamal comes from Morocco.
Our teacher's name is Mrs Delgado.

If you have time, make a 'Facts about us' poster for your classroom.

Revision

In Step 2 you study
- *I agree / I don't agree*
- *I think it's good / I don't think it's good*
- adjectives

so that you can
- understand, ask for and express opinions

My name's Ben Wilson and my favourite subject at school is art. This is my art project. It's a giant chicken. What do you think of it?

1 Key vocabulary *Expressing opinions*

a Read the text. Who's speaking? Can you guess?
Match the five opinions with the photos of Ben's friends.

I think number one is Joe.

Lisa

Jack

Joe

Sadie

Mel

1 It's a bit strange. I don't like it very much.

2 I don't agree. I really like it. I think it's funny.

3 I don't think it's funny. I think it's stupid!

4 I don't know. It's OK, I suppose.

5 I think it's great. I love it.

b 🔊 Listen and check. Write the answers.

1 Joe

c Complete the explanations with *the same* and *different*.

'I agree' means 'we've got _____ opinion'.
'I don't agree' means 'we've got _____ opinions'.

d Complete the sentences with *Joe, Jack*, etc.

1 Sadie doesn't agree with __Joe__. She likes it.
2 Joe and _____ agree. They don't like it.
3 _____ agrees with Sadie. She likes it too.
4 _____ isn't sure. She doesn't know.

Remember!

I think it's funny. I don't think it's funny.
We don't say: ~~I think it isn't funny.~~

2 Vocabulary revision *Adjectives*

Make two lists with these adjectives.

awful silly interesting beautiful boring
exciting brilliant nice good fantastic

1   2

funny   stupid
great   strange

3 Speaking

a **What about you?** Work with a friend and talk about Ben's giant chicken.

A: What do you think of it?

B: I think it's funny.

A: I don't agree. I think it's stupid.

b Make conversations like this.

A: What do you think of <u>Beyoncé</u>?

B: I think <u>she's great. I like her</u>.

Change the <u>underlined</u> words. Use *him / her / it / them*.

4 Listening and speaking
It's a bit strange

a 🔊 Look at the pictures and listen to Jack and Lisa. Have they got the same opinions?

b 🔊 Listen again. Write the adjectives for the pictures.

	Jack	Lisa
1	strange	interesting

c Give your opinion.

> I agree with Jack. I think it's very strange. I don't like it much.

5 Speaking and writing
An opinion poll

Use what you know

Work with the class. Choose a famous person or a TV programme. Write a list of adjectives on the board. Vote for the adjective you agree with. Count the votes. Then make a pie chart and write your results.

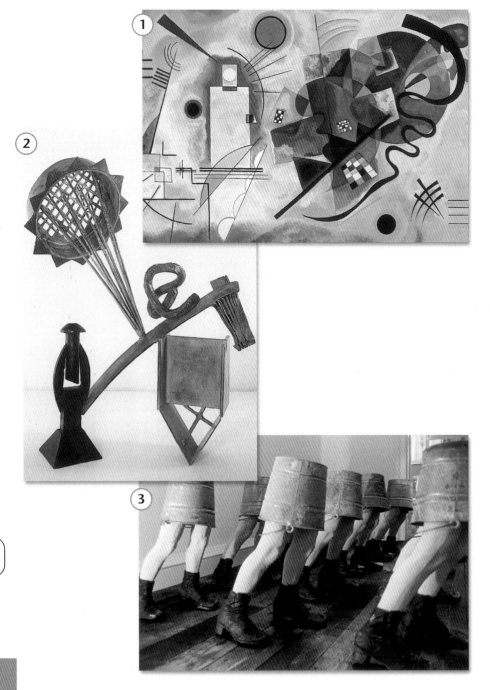

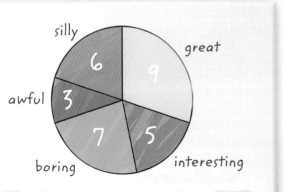

In our class:
9 people think ... is great.
7 people think he/she/it's boring.

In Step 3 you study
- names of interests and activities
- *I like* + *-ing*
- questions with *Do you ... ? Have you got ... ? Can you ... ? Is there ... ?*

so that you can
- talk about things you like and don't like
- ask for and give personal information

1 Key vocabulary *Interests and activities*

a Match the words with the pictures.

computer games   swimming   horror films
using the Internet   going shopping   athletics
going out   meeting friends   astronomy

Listen and check.

b **What about you?** Say at least two things you like and one thing you don't like.

> I like athletics and computer games. I don't like going shopping.

c If you have time, talk about other interests.

> I like volleyball. I like going to the cinema.

Remember!

I read a lot of books. I **like** read**ing**.
I can swim well. I **enjoy** swimm**ing**.

2 Reading and speaking
About Matt

a Look at the questions. Then read the text and find the answers.

1 *I live in Manchester.*

1 Where do you live, Matt?
2 Do you like football?
3 Have you got any other interests?
4 Can you run fast?
5 What's your favourite food?
6 What sort of TV programmes do you like?
7 Is there anything you don't like?

My name's Matt Long and I live in Manchester. Yes, I like football! But my main interests are astronomy and athletics. I can run 100 metres in 13 seconds. My favourite food is pasta. I enjoy watching horror films and programmes about animals. I like music, and I read the newspaper every day. I also like writing letters to our local newspaper. There's one thing I really hate – mobile phones!

b Listen to the conversation with Matt. Then work with a friend and practise.

3 Writing

Imagine you've got a new friend. Write questions about these things.

1 *What's your telephone number?*
2 *Can you play basketball?*

1 address and telephone number
2 abilities
3 brothers and sisters
4 pets
5 interests
6 favourite subjects at school

4 Speaking *Interview a classmate*

Use what you know

Work with a friend. Use sentences from Exercise 3 and ask your friend at least three questions.

Wild Flowers

Chapter 1

Where's Mr Roberts?

It was another boring day at school.

'Tom!' shouted my history teacher. 'Tom!'

'Tom? That's me,' I said. But I said it in an American accent. The class laughed. They think I'm funny, but the teachers don't. They think I'm stupid.

'I suppose you think you're very clever, Tom,' said the history teacher. 'But you're not clever.'

'No, sir,' I said.

Neesha smiled at me. She's my best friend. She understands me. She knows that I don't like history. But I really like science. It's because of Mr Roberts, our science teacher. He's great.

Our next lesson was science, but at 11 o'clock Miss Kay, the head teacher, came into our classroom.

'Good morning, class,' she said. 'Can you all go to the library, please?'

'But we've got science,' I said.

'I know, Tom,' said Miss Kay. 'But there isn't any science today.'

'Where's Mr Roberts?' asked Neesha.

'Mr Roberts is at home,' said the head.

'Why?' I asked. 'Is he ill?'

'No, Tom,' said the head. 'Mr Roberts isn't ill. He doesn't work here any more.'

Suddenly it wasn't a boring day. It was a bad day, a very bad day.

Questions

1 Who is the main character in the story? What can you say about him?
2 Who are Neesha, Mr Roberts and Miss Kay?
3 Tom's class aren't having a science lesson today. Why not?

Extra exercises

1 Choose the right words.

1 a

1 My brother's favourite sports _____ basketball and athletics.
   a are
   b is
   c isn't
2 Bats _____ very big ears.
   a got
   b have got
   c has got
3 _____ any wild elephants in Britain.
   a They're
   b There are
   c There aren't
4 Eva is good at swimming but she _____ dive very well.
   a can
   b can't
   c isn't
5 Our friend Silvana _____ from Italy.
   a come
   b comes
   c coming
6 Jack likes _____ pasta.
   a eat
   b eats
   c eating

2 Read the descriptions. Complete the names of the animals.

1 This animal can fly,
  but it isn't a bird.   b_at_
2 This bird is black and
  white. It can't fly.   p_____
3 This animal has got
  eight legs.   s_____
4 This animal can walk
  on two legs. It can't talk
  but it's very intelligent.   c_____
5 This large wild cat lives
  in Africa and Asia.
  It can run very fast.   c_____
6 This bird usually flies
  at night and sleeps in
  the day.   o_____

3 Match the words in A with the words in B.

1 d

A		B	
1	play	a	shopping
2	read	b	a film
3	go	c	the Internet
4	meet	d	football
5	use	e	the newspaper
6	watch	f	my friends

4 Complete the questions. Then match them with the answers.

1 _Can_ you swim? c   a In Liverpool.
2 _____ you got any pets?   b 01638 427991.
3 _____ you like using a computer?   c Yes, I can.
4 _____ do you live?   d Yes, I love it.
5 _____ your telephone number?   e I think it's boring.
6 _____ do you think of this music?   f No, I haven't.

5 Complete the conversation between four people.

1 d

A: What do you think of this
   book, Chris?
B: I'm not sure. [1]_____
   I can't understand it very well.
A: I love it. [2]_____
C: Yes, [3]_____ It's great.
B: [4]_____ It's sometimes
   quite funny, I suppose, but
   [5]_____ the story's very
   good. What do you think of it,
   David?
D: I don't like it. [6]_____

a I agree with you.
b I think it's awful!
c I don't agree.
d It's a bit strange.
e I don't think
f I think it's brilliant.

6 How do you say these sentences in your language?

1 What do you think of it?
2 It's a bit strange.
3 I think it's stupid.
4 It's OK, I suppose.
5 I don't like it very much.
6 I agree.

Extra reading

I live in New York

What do you know about New York?
Have you got any friends or relatives in the USA?

Hi! My name's Tiffany Morton and I live in New York. Our apartment is in Greenwich Village. I go to East Side Middle School. I'm 14 so I'm in the eighth grade. I travel to school on the subway.

My family is a typical New York family. My grandfather is from Poland and my grandmother is from Italy. My mom's[1] grandparents were Irish. I have an aunt from Puerto Rico and an uncle from Brazil. So my relatives speak five different languages!

My dad's a sculptor and my mom's an art teacher. I suppose that's why I'm interested in art. There are some fantastic museums and galleries in New York. My favorite[2] is the Museum of Modern Art.

Another of my favorite places is Central Park. It's four kilometres long and there are 75,000 trees. I go rollerblading there with my friends and, in the summer, we swim at the pool after school. I like going to the theater[3] on Broadway but it's very expensive.

People think New York is dangerous, but I don't agree. It's certainly a busy, noisy place. After all, eight million people live here. Why don't you come and visit us?

American	British
[1]mom	mum
[2]favorite	favourite
[3]theater	theatre

ABOUT NEW YORK

Did you know that the city's nickname is 'the Big Apple'?

Task

Read the text and find the following things.
1 The name of a part of New York.
2 The names of four different countries.
3 At least two of Tiffany's interests.
4 Her parents' jobs.
5 Two things you can do in Central Park.
6 The population of New York.

2 A slice of life

In Step 1 you study
- present simple

so that you can
- talk about your daily life
- describe what other people do

1 Presentation
He lives in the Antarctic

a What can you say about the photos?

b 🔊 Cover the text and listen to Nick. Does he talk about all these things?

1 work 2 food 3 travel 4 clothes
5 school 6 free time 7 the weather

c 🔊 Listen and read about Nick's life in the Antarctic. Check your answers in 1b.

My name's Nick Bowen. I'm a scientist. I work for the British Antarctic Survey. I study the climate and the stars. I live at the Halley Research Station.

Our food comes by ship. It arrives twice a year, in March and October.

We travel on skidoos or we ski. We've also got five small planes. But we don't travel by plane in the winter because it's dark all the time.

Outside we wear special clothes and big boots, and sunglasses when it's sunny.

In our free time we play a lot of games. We play cards. We sing and I play my guitar. Every Saturday we have a party and a special meal.

We can't watch TV but we've got a lot of videos and every week someone chooses a film. It's always very cold, of course, but in the summer we sometimes go swimming and diving.

The Antarctic is a fascinating and beautiful place. I love it.

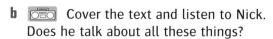

d Answer the questions about Nick's life.

1 He's a scientist. He works for the British Antarctic Survey.

1 What's Nick's job?
2 What does he study?
3 Where does he live?
4 When does their food arrive?
5 How does Nick travel?
6 Why doesn't he travel by plane in the winter?
7 What does he wear when he's outside?
8 What does he do in his free time?
9 Does he watch TV?
10 Does he like living in the Antarctic?

2 Key grammar *Present simple*

Complete the table.

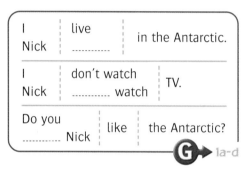

I Nick	live	in the Antarctic.
I Nick	don't watch .... watch	TV.
Do you .... Nick	like	the Antarctic?

G 1a-d

3 Practice

a Complete these sentences with *I / you* or *he*.

1 What do ..you.. do in your free time?
2 .... usually wears glasses.
3 Does .... have cereal for breakfast?
4 .... don't like travelling by plane.
5 .... doesn't go to school by bus.
6 .... sometimes play cards at the weekend.
7 What sort of food do .... like?
8 Where does .... live?

> **Try this!**
> How many words can you think of for things you can see in the Antarctic?
> *penguins*

b Test a friend

Write another sentence for 3a. Leave a blank for *I / you / he*. Can your friend complete the sentence?

.... *walks to school.*

4 Key pronunciation /s/ /z/ /ɪz/

Listen and repeat the verbs.

1 /s/ works takes eats
2 /z/ comes wears travels
3 /ɪz/ watches chooses uses

Now listen and put these verbs in the right group.

lives dances likes sits finishes arrives

5 Writing and speaking

a What about you? Write at least three questions for your friends about the topics in 1b.

Do you wear your baseball cap every day? How do you travel to school?

b Work with a friend. Ask and answer your questions.

> Do you wear your baseball cap every day?

> Yes, I do.

c Tell the class about your friend.

> Carlos wears his baseball cap every day.

6 Writing *Life in my country*

Use what you know

Think about the sort of life you and your friends have. Write a short description for someone who lives in another country.

My name's Carlos. I live in Spain and I go to school in Valencia. We don't wear a uniform at school. In our free time, we ...

G *When you see this, look at the Grammar notes at the back of the Workbook.*

In Step 2 you study
- frequency adverbs
- expressions of frequency

so that you can
- talk about how often you do things
- write a questionnaire about your favourite pastimes

1 Presentation

How often do you play?

a What can you say about the photo?

b 🔊 Close your book and listen to Lisa and Sadie. Is Sadie a computer addict?

Sadie spends a lot of time on her computer. Lisa's asking her some questions about it.

LISA: Hey, Sadie, let's do this questionnaire. 'Computer games. Are you addicted?'

SADIE: OK, then.

LISA: First question: Do you play computer games every day?

SADIE: Not every day, no.

LISA: How often do you play?

SADIE: Five or six times a week, I suppose.

LISA: That's nearly every day! Next question: Do you often play for a long time?

SADIE: Yes, I do.

LISA: Do you always try to beat your top score?

SADIE: Usually, but not always.

LISA: And, if you can't play, do you feel anxious?

SADIE: Anxious? No, of course I don't.

LISA: Are you sure? Never?

SADIE: Well, sometimes, perhaps.

LISA: I think you've got a problem, Sadie. You're addicted!

c 🔊 Listen again and follow in your book. Are these sentences true or false? Correct the false sentences.

1 False. She doesn't play every day.

1 Sadie plays computer games every day.
2 She enjoys playing computer games.
3 She often plays them.
4 She usually plays five or six times a day.
5 She never plays for a long time.
6 She always tries to beat her top score.
7 She sometimes feels anxious if she can't play.
8 Sadie isn't addicted to computer games.

2 Key grammar

Frequency adverbs

Complete the list of frequency adverbs. How do you say these words in your language?

	always		
I	u_____		enjoy computer games.
	o_____		
	sometimes		
	n_____		

G ➔ 25a-b

3 Practice

a **What about you?** Make true sentences. Use *always, often,* etc.

1 I never sing in the shower.

1 sing in the shower
2 argue with my friends
3 read poems
4 wear my socks in bed
5 worry about the future

b Work with a friend. Ask and answer at least two questions.

A: Do you argue with your friends?
B: Yes, sometimes.
A: Do you sing in the shower?
B: No, never.

4 Key vocabulary
Expressions of frequency

How often do you	read poems?
	travel by bus?
	tidy your room?

Once		day.
Twice		week.
Three times	a	month.
Four times		year.

Every day.
Not very often.
Never.

What about you? Make at least two questions with *How often … ?* Then ask and answer.

> How often do you tidy your room?

> Once a year!

5 Speaking

Work with a friend. Ask him/her the questions in the conversation in 1b.

> Do you play computer games every day?

> No, I don't.

Is your friend addicted to computer games?

6 Reading and speaking
Teenagers' lifestyles

a Read the information about teenagers in the USA. Are they very different from teenagers in your country?

Teenagers all over the world agree that their favourite pastimes are watching and playing sport and listening to music.

A recent survey showed that the most popular sports activities in the USA are swimming, basketball, jogging, bowling, football, baseball, rollerblading, tennis and volleyball.

American teenagers also like using the Internet, playing computer games, reading books and magazines, going to the cinema, playing cards and games, and spending time with their friends and families.

b Read the text again. Find these things.

1 Four things that you do in a team.
2 Four things that you can do at home.
3 Four things that you usually do outside.

c **What about you?** Use words from the text and make at least two sentences about your pastimes.

I go rollerblading. I play tennis.
I like spending time with my friends.

> **Remember!**
>
> I **go** swimming/jogging/bowling/rollerblading.
> I **play** basketball/football/baseball/volleyball/tennis.

7 Writing and speaking *Questionnaire*

Use what you know

Choose at least four activities and write a questionnaire. Ask a friend and tick the answers.

How often do you	use the Internet	go jogging	play volleyball	listen to music?
every day				
two or three times a week	✓			
about once a week				
not very often				
never				

If you have time, make sentences about your friend. *Selma doesn't often go jogging.*

In Step 3 you study
- names of everyday routines
- link words

so that you can
- talk about everyday routines
- write about your average day

1 Key vocabulary
Everyday routines

⏱ Match the words with the pictures. You've got two minutes!

wash   get dressed   get undressed
get home   get ready for school   get up
wake up   go to bed   go to sleep
have a drink   have a shower

🔊 Listen and check.

2 Reading *Matt's routines*

a Read about Matt's day. Find three verbs that aren't in the pictures in Exercise 1.

Matt's alarm clock rings at half past seven. Matt usually listens to the radio before he gets up. Then, after about ten minutes, he gets up and has a shower. After that, he has a drink and some toast. Then, after breakfast, he gets ready for school. Matt goes to bed about ten and he usually reads before he goes to sleep.

b Read the text again, then look at these sentences. Only one sentence is right. Can you find it?

1 Matt gets up and then he listens to the radio.
2 He has breakfast. After that, he has a shower.
3 He gets ready for school and then he has some toast.
4 He has a drink before he goes to school.
5 He reads before he goes to bed.

Remember!
Link words
before   after   then   after that

3 Listening *Song*

a 🔊 Listen to the song. Do the singers like Monday?

b 🔊 Listen again. Match the words in A with the words in B and make sentences from the song.

A		B	
1	The alarm clock	a	to get up.
2	I can't	b	begins.
3	Another week	c	is burning.
4	I don't want	d	rings.
5	Your toast	e	a mess.
6	Don't forget	f	wake up.
7	Your hair's	g	your bus pass.

4 Writing *An average day*

Use what you know

Write about your average day. Use vocabulary from Steps 1, 2 and 3 and the 'link words'.

My day usually starts at seven o'clock. I have a shower and then I get dressed. After that, I have a hot chocolate and some cereal.

Chapter 2

Tom wants to find out

The class went to the library, but I wanted to find out about Mr Roberts. I always want to find out about things. That's why I like science. So I walked back to the science room. Miss Kay, the head, was there with another teacher, Mrs Price. I hid outside the door and listened.

'This is very bad,' said Miss Kay. 'You know that all the exam papers came from London this week.'

'Yes,' said Mrs Price.

'And,' said Miss Kay, 'no one sees them before the exam.'

Mrs Price said 'yes' again.

'All the exam papers are in a cupboard in my office,' said Miss Kay. 'But this morning the cupboard was open and I looked inside and …'

This was exciting, I thought.

'… the science paper wasn't there,' Miss Kay said.

'So what did you do?' Mrs Price asked.

'I came in here. The exam paper was in Mr Roberts' desk.'

I ran back to the library. 'They say Mr Roberts took an exam paper,' I told Neesha.

'That's terrible,' she said.

'But I don't believe it,' I said. 'So we're going to find out what really happened.'

'Don't be silly,' said Neesha. 'We can't do anything.'

'Yes, we can,' I said. 'The head thinks Mr Roberts took the exam paper. But I think someone put it there.'

'But who?' asked Neesha. 'And why?'

'That's what we're going to find out,' I told her.

Questions

1 Why did Tom go to the science room?
2 According to Miss Kay, what happened this morning?
3 Does Tom think that Mr Roberts took the paper?

Extra exercises

1 Choose the right words.

1 My friends _____ a lot of magazines.
  a read
  b reads
  c reading

2 Sadie _____ a shower in the evening.
  a usually have
  b usually hasn't
  c doesn't usually have

3 Peter and I never _____ home from school before 5 o'clock.
  a get
  b don't get
  c doesn't get

4 After breakfast, Jack _____ ready for school.
  a get
  b gets
  c goes

5 _____ Kate like spending time with her family?
  a Is
  b Does
  c Do

6 How often _____ by plane?
  a you travel
  b are you travel
  c do you travel

2 Complete the conversations with *do, does, don't* or *doesn't*.

A: [1]_____ the London train stop at this station?
B: Yes, it [2]_____ .
A: What time [3]_____ it arrive?
B: Sorry, I [4]_____ know.

A: How often [5]_____ Martina go to the sports club?
B: About three times a month.
A: [6]_____ you often play basketball together?
B: No, we [7]_____ . Martina [8]_____ like it much.

3 Where do people usually do these activities? Write the words with *play* or *go* and make two lists.

football   computer games   jogging   cards   bowling
baseball   rollerblading

Outside	Inside
play football	

4 Write sentences. Put the adverbs in the right place.

1 Karen doesn't usually go to bed late.

1 Karen / not go / to bed late (*usually*)
2 I / read / in bed (*never*)
3 Richard / have / a drink / when he / get / home (*sometimes*)
4 We / not wake up / before 7 o'clock (*often*)
5 Julie / drink / hot chocolate ? (*always*)
6 you / have / a shower before breakfast ? (*usually*)
7 Matt / not burn / his toast (*usually*)
8 your food / arrive / by ship ? (*always*)

5 Change the underlined words. Use the expressions in the list.

four times a week   three times a day   every day
twice a day   once a month   twice a year

1 Diana reads her email three times a day.

1 Diana reads her email <u>at 9 o'clock, at 1 o'clock and at 4 o'clock</u>.
2 The cinema is open <u>from Monday to Sunday</u>.
3 Frank goes to the dentist <u>in February and July</u>.
4 They have maths lessons <u>on Monday, Tuesday, Thursday and Friday</u>.
5 We meet <u>on the first Saturday of every month</u>.
6 Suzanne cleans her teeth <u>after breakfast and before she goes to bed</u>.

6 How do you say these sentences in your language?

1 What do you do in your free time?
2 Are you sure?
3 Let's go home. – OK, then.
4 Do you eat insects? – No, of course I don't.
5 Your hair is a mess.
6 How often do you clean your teeth?

Life and culture

Making music

Do you know the names of any musical instruments?
Do you play a musical instrument?

People in Britain love listening to music, and they enjoy making music too.

Thousands of schoolchildren play a musical instrument, and they like classical music as well as pop! They have music lessons at school and at home. If they're very good, they can join the National Children's Orchestra (the NCO). Its members come from all over Britain and they're all under 14.

There are training courses twice a year – usually at Easter and in the summer holidays. The students practise every day and, at the end of the week, they give a concert. But they don't work all the time. They can go swimming, do sport and they always have a lot of fun.

The orchestra gives concerts in London, Birmingham and Liverpool, and its musicians sometimes appear on radio and television. They make CDs too.

One member of the orchestra told us, 'For me, it's a different world. I love being part of a real orchestra. At the end of the training courses, I never want to go home!'

Task
Read the text, then answer these questions.
1 Do people in Britain like making music?
2 What sort of music do British schoolchildren like?
3 What does NCO mean?
4 How old are the members of the NCO?
5 How often do they have training courses?
6 What do they do at the end of the course?
7 Can people see them on TV?

ABOUT ORCHESTRAS
A full orchestra has got about 90 musicians and four different sections: strings, woodwind, brass and percussion.

Language summary

1 There is/are

We use *there is* with singular nouns and *there are* with plural nouns. In a list, we use *there is* if the first noun is singular: *There's a kitchen, a living room and two bedrooms.*

> *Affirmative*
> There's a hole in my shoe.
> There are some crisps in the cupboard.
>
> *Negative*
> There isn't a TV in our classroom.
> There aren't any posters.
>
> *Questions and answers*
> Is there a bus stop near here?
> Yes, there is. / No, there isn't.
> Are there any trains on Sunday?
> Yes, there are. / No, there aren't.
>
> *Remember!*
> There are **some** ...
> There aren't **any** ...
> Are there **any** ... ?

Check that you can

* use *there's/are*.

Make complete sentences.

1 .... two emails for you.
2 .... a famous cathedral in Barcelona.
3 .... an owl in that tree.
4 .... a gym, a swimming pool and two tennis courts.
5 .... some sandwiches and some apples.
6 .... 26 letters in the English alphabet.

2 can/can't

We describe abilities with *can/can't* + verb.

Affirmative and negative

I/You/He/She It/We/They	can can't	run very fast. swim well.

Questions and answers

Can	you/he/she it/they	use sign language?
Yes, No,	I/you/he/she/it/we/they	can. can't.
can't = cannot		

Check that you can

2.1 ● describe different abilities.

Make true sentences. Use *can* or *can't*.

1 I .... swim well.
2 Cats .... see in the dark.
3 I .... speak Arabic.
4 Penguins .... fly.
5 Matt .... run fast.
6 I .... play the piano.

2.2 ● ask and answer questions about abilities.

Make questions for your sentences in 2.1, then ask and answer.

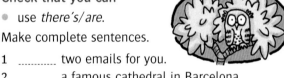

3 have/has got

We use *have/has got* to describe:

* our possessions ● our families
* how we feel ● our appearance

Affirmative and negative

I/You/We/They	've haven't	got	a car. seven sisters.
He/She/It	's hasn't		a headache. big ears.

Questions and answers

Have you/they Has he/she/it	got	long legs?
Yes, No,	I/you/we/they	have. haven't.
Yes, No,	he/she/it	has. hasn't.
I've got = I have got He's got = He has got haven't = have not hasn't = has not		

Check that you can

3.1 ● describe possessions and appearance.

Make true sentences with the correct form of *have got*.

1 I .... a pen friend.
2 Matt .... long hair.
3 Sadie .... a computer.
4 I .... an alarm clock.
5 Cheetahs .... very powerful legs.
6 Nick Bowen .... an interesting job.

3.2 ● ask questions with *have/has got*.

Make questions for the sentences in 3.1, then ask and answer.

4 Subject and object pronouns

Subject	Object
I	me
You	you
He	him
She	her
It	it
We	us
You	you
They	them

Object pronouns always go after the verb:

*We never win. They always beat **us**.*
*It's awful. I don't like **it**.*

Check that you can

- use object pronouns.

Complete the sentences.

1 Cheetahs are fantastic. I love
....

2 Where's my anorak? Can you
see .... ?

3 Matt's a very good player.
I never beat ....

4 I can't do this. Can you help
.... ?

5 What's Lisa like? Can you
describe .... ?

6 What did you say?
I can't hear ....

7 We've got some tickets.
Come with ....

5 like + -ing

After *like, love, enjoy, hate* we usually use a noun, a pronoun or a verb + *-ing*.

	like	chocolate.
	love	it.
I	don't like	running.
	enjoy	learning
	hate	English.

See Spelling notes, page 143.

Check that you can

- describe your likes and dislikes.

Make true sentences with *like, love, enjoy, hate* and verb + *-ing*. Use:

watch horror films   do sport   dance
have tests at school   get up early

6 Present simple

We use the present simple to describe:

- habits and routines: *I go to bed at ten thirty.*
- things that are generally true: *It rains a lot in England.*
- our opinions, likes and dislikes: *I agree. I don't think it's funny.*
  Matt hates mobile phones.

Affirmative

I/You/We/They	live	
He/She/It	lives	in Antarctica.

Negative

I/You/We/They	don't live	
He/She/It	doesn't live	here.

Questions and answers

Do you/they Does he/she/it		live here?
Yes, No,	I/you/we/they	do. don't.
Yes, No,	he/she/it	does. doesn't.
don't = do not doesn't = does not		

See Spelling notes, page 143.

Check that you can

- use the present simple.

Put the words in the right order and make sentences.

1 the / cards / Nick / in / evening / plays
2 does / work ? / where / she
3 like / spiders / don't / I
4 you / get up ? / do / when

5 in / comes / ship / October / the
6 Sadie / meat / eat / doesn't
7 and / astronomy / likes / Matt / athletics
8 agree / Lisa / don't / Ben / and

7 Frequency adverbs and expressions of frequency

always   usually   often   sometimes   never

Check that you can

7.1 - talk about habits and routines.

Make complete sentences.

1 Joe doesn't always have lunch in the canteen.

1 Joe / not have lunch in the canteen (*always*)
2 We / not read magazines in our English lessons (*often*)
3 Mike / cook the dinner ? (*always*)

4 I / dream about school (*sometimes*)
5 Matt / goes rollerblading (*never*)
6 Mel / not walk to school (*usually*)

How often do you tidy your room?
Once a month. Three times a day. Every day.
Twice a week. Four times a year. Every week.

Check that you can

7.2 - say how often you do things.

Make true sentences.

I wash my hair two or three times a week.

Vocabulary

Adjectives
awful
beautiful
boring
brilliant
exciting
fantastic
fascinating
funny
good
great
interesting
nice
silly
strange
stupid

Expressing an opinion
I agree (with you).
I don't agree.
I don't like it (very) much.
I don't think it's funny.
I (really) like it.
I think it's great.

Interests and activities
astronomy
athletics
computer games
going jogging
going out
going rollerblading
going shopping
going to the cinema
horror films
meeting friends
playing basketball
playing cards
reading
swimming
using the Internet

Daily life
clothes
food
free time
school
the weather
travel (n.)
work (n.)

Everyday routines
(to) get dressed
(to) get home
(to) get ready for school
(to) get undressed
(to) get up
(to) go to bed
(to) go to sleep
(to) have a drink
(to) have a shower
(to) listen to the radio
(to) wake up
(to) wash

Link words
after
after that
before
then

Expressions
How often do you ... ?
I go three times a year.
I love it.
It's OK, I suppose.
Of course I don't.
OK, then.
What sort of programmes ... ?

Study skills 1 Using your book

Remember to

- look at the 'aims box' at the beginning of the 'steps' in each unit.
- read each 'step' when it is finished.
- use the lists at the back of the book.

And don't forget to ask your teacher for help!

How well do you know your book? Answer these questions. You've got five minutes!

1 How many pages are there in a unit?
2 Where can you find a list of irregular verbs?
3 Write the names of four of the teenagers in *Messages*.
4 Where can you learn to describe everyday routines? Look at the map at the front of the book, then find the right page.
5 Where can you revise the grammar of Units 3 and 4?
6 Find at least one photo of London. What page is it on?

How's it going?

- ## Your rating

Look again at pages 22–23. For each section give yourself a star rating:

Good ☆ ☆ ☆   Not bad ☆ ☆   I can't remember much ☆

- ## Vocabulary

Choose two titles in the Vocabulary list, then close your book. How many words can you remember for each topic?

- ## Test a friend

Look again at Units 1 and 2. Think of at least two questions, then ask a friend.

> Has Matt got a mobile phone?
> What's the weather like in Antarctica?

- ## Correcting mistakes

Can you correct these mistakes?

1 ~~I think is not funny.~~ *I don't think it's funny.*
2 ~~Sadie love computer games.~~
3 ~~I no like swim.~~

- ## Your Workbook

Complete the Learning Diaries for Units 1 and 2.

Coursework 1 — My window on the world

Read Matt's newsletter, then write a newsletter about your country. Use pictures and photos too.

Life in Britain

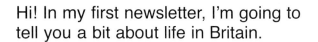

Hi! In my first newsletter, I'm going to tell you a bit about life in Britain.

There are three countries in Britain – England, Scotland and Wales – and there are 58 million people. The people are a mixture of different nationalities and ethnic groups. For example, 2.3 million people are Asian.

London is the capital city. The population is about seven million. The government meets at the Houses of Parliament, and the prime minister lives at 10 Downing Street.

In Britain school starts about nine o'clock and finishes about three thirty. People usually start work between eight and nine and finish between five and six.

A lot of my friends do sport in their free time. The British are great sports fans.

At the weekend, people here like going to the cinema, shopping or just staying at home.

My parents love gardening, and my mum goes to an evening class once a week. She's learning Spanish at the moment.

Module 2

In the past

In Module 2 you study

Grammar

- Past simple of *be*
- Past simple: regular and irregular verbs

Vocabulary

- Numbers and dates
- Holidays
- Jobs
- Past time expressions

so that you can

- Say when things happened in the past
- Invent your own 'world record'
- Talk about events in the past
- Write about a holiday
- Tell a short story
- Ask for and give information about the past
- Make a quiz about the past
- Write an interview about a star's career

Wild Flowers

Chapter 3 – Don't ask questions!
Chapter 4 – Money or flowers?

Life and culture

The garden-chair pilot
Making movies

Coursework 2

Biographies
You write about famous people in your country.

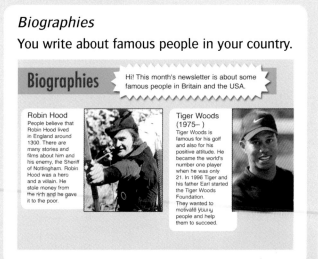

Biographies

Hi! This month's newsletter is about some famous people in Britain and the USA.

Robin Hood
People believe that Robin Hood lived in England around 1300. There are many stories and films about him and his enemy, the Sheriff of Nottingham. Robin Hood was a hero and a villain. He stole money from the rich and he gave it to the poor.

Tiger Woods (1975–)
Tiger Woods is famous for his golf and also for his positive attitude. He became the world's number one player when he was only 21. In 1996 Tiger and his father Earl started the Tiger Woods Foundation. They wanted to motivate young people and help them to succeed.

What's it about?

What can you say about the pictures?

Now match the pictures with sentences 1–5.

1 She lived with 6,069 scorpions!
2 We went to France last summer.
3 In town one day Frank stole a horse ...
4 Why did they go to Hollywood?
5 I worked on *Lord of the Rings*.

ad of Billy Magee

3 Stories

STEP 1

In Step 1 you study
- numbers and dates
- past simple (affirmative): *be*, regular verbs

so that you can
- say when things happened in the past
- invent your own 'world record'

1 Key vocabulary
Numbers and dates

a How many of these can you say?

13   30   125.2
3,978   462,510   1,000,000
9th November 1800
21st July 1999
3rd January 2005

🔊 Listen and say the numbers and dates.

b **Test a friend** Write a number, then say it to a friend.

> Seven hundred and thirty one thousand, eight hundred and sixty-five.

Your friend writes the number.
731,865

2 Key pronunciation 13 30 13th

🔊 Listen and repeat these numbers.

13 30 30th

🔊 Now listen and write the number you hear.

1 18 80 18th *80*
2 16 60 16th
3 14 40 14th
4 17 70 17th
5 15 50 15th
6 19 90 19th

Say the right answers.

> 1   eighty

3 Presentation
He walked backwards

a What can you say about the pictures?

b Match the sentences with the pictures.

1 Seb Clover sailed across the Atlantic on his own when he was 15 years old.
2 They were born on 14th January 1998.
3 Malena Hassan, the 'Scorpion Queen', lived in a glass cage with 6,069 scorpions for 36 days.
4 In 1978 Walter Robinson walked across the English Channel. He used special 'water shoes'.
5 Anthony Thornton walked backwards for 24 hours. He travelled at an average speed of 6.4 kilometres an hour.

🔊 Listen and check.

c Are these sentences true or false? Correct the false sentences.

1 Seb's parents were on the boat with him.
2 Malena was in a glass cage for a week.
3 6,069 scorpions lived there with her.
4 Walter travelled by boat.
5 Anthony walked 6.4 kilometres.

4 Key grammar *Past simple:* was, were

What's the past tense of *am*, *is* and *are*?

I/He/She/It	was	15 years old yesterday.
We/You/They	were	born in 1998.

G ➤ 4a

5 Practice

a Complete the sentences with *was* or *were*.

1 They _were_ born in 1998.
2 The scorpions _____ very hungry.
3 Walter _____ cold and tired.
4 Seb Clover _____ very young.
5 Walter's special shoes _____ amazing.
6 It _____ my birthday yesterday! I _____ fifteen.

b **What about you?** Talk to your friends.

> I was born on 10th July. What about you, Paulo?

> I was born on 21st November. What about you, Rosa?

6 Key grammar
Past simple: regular verbs

Complete the two lists, then complete the explanation.

Present	Past
live	lived
1 _____	sailed
2 _____	travelled
walk	3 _____
use	4 _____

Regular verbs in the past simple end in _____ .
See Spelling notes, page 143.

G ➔ 2a, c

7 Practice

Complete the sentences with the past simple of verbs in Exercise 6.

1 Walter _walked_ from Dover to Calais.
2 Columbus _____ across the Atlantic.
3 Phineas Fogg _____ around the world in eighty days.
4 Romeo and Juliet _____ in a city called Verona.
5 When Seb was at sea, he _____ a special telephone.
6 Robert Scott _____ to the South Pole.

Try this!

Steve Briers talked continuously for nearly ten minutes. What's so special about that?
sdrawkcabdeklateh

8 Listening and speaking *It's a record!*

a Match the verbs with the pictures.

play stay dive live walk

b 🔊 Listen and find the right picture. Write the number of the picture.

c Make complete sentences about the pictures.

1 *He walked to Paris on his hands.*

1 He / on his hands
2 He / 21 years
3 They / 28 hours
4 She / 160 metres
5 She / three minutes and 26 seconds

9 Writing and speaking *My world record*

Use what you know

Invent a new world record and tell the class.

> In 2004 I walked from Rome to Madrid on my hands. I finished the journey in 46 days.

Vote for the most interesting idea.

In Step 2 you study
- past simple (affirmative): irregular verbs

so that you can
- talk about events in the past
- write about a holiday

1 Key vocabulary *Holidays*

🔊 Listen and say the words.
Find the things in the photos.
Which things aren't in the photos?

caravan   tent   sleeping bag   sea
plane   hotel   ferry   campsite
beach   rucksack

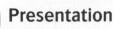

2 Presentation
We went to France

a 🔊 Close your book and listen to Matt's story.
What was in Matt's sleeping bag?

We usually go to France in the summer. We stay at a campsite. We take our caravan and we get the ferry from Plymouth to Roscoff. Then we drive to the south.

Last summer my cousin Jack came with us, so we took a tent for me and Jack. We got the ferry as usual and went to a campsite near the sea.

One morning my mum came into our tent with a drink and, suddenly, she said 'Matt! Don't move!' There was a scorpion in my sleeping bag.

I was quite scared, but Jack pushed the scorpion into his shoe with a magazine. Then he took it outside. He ran across the road and put it under the trees. My parents said 'You're a hero, Jack!'

We had a great holiday but, after that, everyone looked in their sleeping bags before they went to sleep.

(3)

b 📻 Listen again and follow in your book. Then complete the sentences. Who was it?

1 <u>Matt, Jack and Matt's parents</u> went to France last summer.
2 _____ went on holiday with his cousin, Matt.
3 _____ slept in a tent.
4 _____ slept in the caravan.
5 _____ saw the scorpion first.
6 _____ was scared.
7 _____ took the scorpion outside.
8 _____ put it under the trees.
9 _____ said 'You're a hero!'

3 Key grammar

Past simple: irregular verbs

Complete the table with verbs from the story.

Present	Past
come	came
get	1 _____
go	2 _____
have	3 _____
put	put
run	4 _____
say	5 _____
see	saw
sleep	slept
take	6 _____

G► 3a

4 Practice

a Complete the sentences with verbs from the table.

1 Jack <u>took</u> his sleeping bag with him.
2 Matt's family _____ to France last summer.
3 They _____ the ferry in Plymouth.
4 Jack and Matt _____ in their tent.
5 They _____ to sleep very late.
6 They _____ a great time.

b **Test a friend** Use a verb from the table and make another sentence about a holiday. Can your friend find the right verb?

We _____ breakfast in our tent.

5 Reading *Last summer*

⏱ Read the story and choose the right words. You've got five minutes! 1b

Last summer we ¹_____ to Greece on holiday. We ²_____ at a campsite near ³_____ . The weather ⁴_____ great. It was hot and ⁵_____ all the time. We went ⁶_____ in the sea every day and we ate a lot of ⁷_____ . We also went on a boat trip and ⁸_____ some dolphins. We ⁹_____ a fantastic time. I want to ¹⁰_____ there again next year.

1 a stayed   b went   c came
2 a got   b stayed   c went
3 a the sea   b Madrid   c my house
4 a is   b were   c was
5 a cold   b sunny   c windy
6 a rollerblading   b shopping   c swimming
7 a dogs   b scorpions   c ice cream
8 a see   b saw   c sea
9 a had   b were   c did
10 a going   b went   c go

📻 Listen and check.

6 Writing *Holidays*

Use what you know

Write about a real or an imaginary holiday.

Last summer I went to Palma. I stayed at my aunt's house.

Write 30–40 words.

The Ballad of Billy Magee

1 Presentation
I didn't do it

a What can you say about the pictures?

b 📻 Listen and read the poem. Who killed the sheriff?

c Are these sentences true, false or 'we don't know'?

1 Billy's parents were only together for a short time.
2 His mother didn't stay with her children.
3 Life was easy when Frank and Billy were young.
4 Billy's brother wasn't an honest person.
5 Frank didn't steal Judge Lee's money.
6 Frank didn't shoot the sheriff.
7 The judge didn't believe Billy.
8 Frank visited Billy in prison.

Billy was born on a windy night
In a town called Sante Fé.
But his parents weren't in love for long
And his father didn't stay.
Life was hard when Billy was young.
He didn't go to school.
He played in the streets with his brother, Frank.
But Frank was cold and cruel.
In town one day Frank stole a horse.
It belonged to Judge John Lee.
When the sheriff came, Frank shot him dead.
'It was Billy,' he said. 'Not me!'
'I didn't kill him!' poor Billy said.
'I wasn't even there!'
But the judge didn't want to listen.
And Frank? He didn't care.
Billy went to prison for a long, long time.
He died in a prison bed.
And the town heard a voice in the wind that night.
'I didn't do it!' Billy said.

2 Key grammar
Past simple: negative

a What's the negative form of *was* and *were*?

Billy	wasn't	there.
His parents	weren't	together for long.

G→4a

b Do we form the negative of regular and irregular verbs in the same way?

Billy	didn't	kill the sheriff.
		go to school.

G→2a, 3b

3 Practice

Choose the right words and make true sentences.

1 *The judge didn't believe Billy.*

1 The judge (*believed / didn't believe*) Billy.
2 Billy (*was / wasn't*) a bad man.
3 His mother and father (*were / weren't*) together for long.
4 The horse (*belonged / didn't belong*) to Frank.
5 Frank (*killed / didn't kill*) the sheriff.
6 Frank (*went / didn't go*) to prison.
7 The judged (*listened / didn't listen*) to Billy.

4 Speaking and writing *Frank's confession*

Use what you know

Imagine you're Frank. Your brother is dead and now you're sorry. Share your ideas and then write Frank's story.

Life wasn't easy when I was young. My father left when I was three. Billy and I didn't go ...

Don't ask questions!

Neesha and I knew where Mr Roberts lived, and so we went to see him after school. He didn't say much and he looked very unhappy.

'I didn't take the paper,' he told us. 'I told the head, but she didn't believe me.'

'We believe you,' I told him.

'Thanks,' he said, 'but there's nothing you can do. Go home.'

So I went home, but I did something. I wrote a question on a big piece of paper. The next day I put it on the notice board:

DID YOU SEE ANYONE GO INTO THE SCIENCE ROOM ON WEDNESDAY BEFORE 9 AM?

That evening someone sent me a text message. It read: 'Do you want to see your cat again? Then don't ask questions.'

I took it to Mum. 'It's a joke,' she said. 'It's from one of your friends.'

'But where is Maggie?' I asked. Maggie is our cat.

'Maggie's out,' she said. 'Cats often go out for hours.'

I went outside and shouted for Maggie. Then I put some food in her bowl. But she didn't come home.

I rang Neesha. 'I know the text message wasn't from a friend,' I said.

'How?' she asked.

'Because we don't use whole words when we text. And someone has got our cat.'

'Who?' she asked.

'I don't know,' I said. 'But I'm going to find out.'

Questions

1 Why was Mr Roberts unhappy?
2 What did Tom put on the notice board? Why?
3 How did Tom know that the text message wasn't from a friend?
4 Why was Tom worried about Maggie?

Extra exercises

1 Choose the right words.

1 Julie _____ late for her guitar lesson yesterday.
   a is
   b was
   c were

2 His parents _____ in Madrid.
   a born
   b are born
   c were born

3 I _____ some nice shoes when I went shopping.
   a saw
   b said
   c seen

4 Tony _____ in New York for eight years.
   a loves
   b liked
   c lived

5 It _____ cold last week.
   a isn't
   b wasn't
   c didn't

6 We _____ a very good time at the party.
   a haven't
   b haven't got
   c didn't have

2 Complete the sentences with *was, wasn't, were* or *weren't*.

1 I had a cup of tea and an apple at lunchtime. I _____ very hungry.

2 Simon and his father _____ in Australia last year. They stayed in Sydney and Melbourne.

3 There _____ a swimming pool at our hotel, but we didn't use it very often.

4 We didn't sleep well. The hotel was noisy and our beds _____ comfortable.

5 My glasses _____ in my bag last night but they aren't here now.

6 Sally and Tim _____ on the train this morning. I think they got the bus.

3 Complete the sentences. Use the past simple form of the verbs.

1 They *sailed* in a boat from Greece to Turkey. (*sail*)

2 Annie had breakfast and then she _____ ready for school. (*get*)

3 My cousins _____ in Asia for six weeks last year. (*travel*)

4 We went to a campsite. We _____ in a hotel. (*not stay*)

5 It was grey and cloudy, so I _____ an umbrella with me. (*take*)

6 I _____ Charlie at the sports club yesterday. (*not see*)

7 Dad _____ , 'I've got some fish and chips for lunch!' (*say*)

8 Ben and Laura _____ to our party on Saturday. (*not come*)

4 Complete the sentences with holiday vocabulary.

1 In summer there are always a lot of tents at the c_ampsite_ .

2 They travelled across the English Channel on a f_____ .

3 You can carry your things in a r_____ .

4 I slept in a s_____ in my tent.

5 He went from London to Paris by p_____ . The trip took about an hour.

6 Jane's hotel was near the b_____ , so she went swimming in the sea every morning.

7 When we go away, we usually take our c_____ . We can sleep, wash and cook inside and it's very comfortable.

5 Read the text and choose the right word for each space.

Cathy started skiing when she went [1]_____ holiday to Germany with her friend Sonia. They travelled [2]_____ train and stayed in a big hotel in the mountains. At first Cathy [3]_____ a bit anxious because she [4]_____ know how to ski, but she learned very fast. [5]_____ two lessons with Sonia, she was fine. After that, the girls went [6]_____ together every day. Cathy loved it. At the end of the week she didn't [7]_____ to come home.

		a		b		c
1	a	to	b	on	c	in
2	a	in	b	with	c	by
3	a	get	b	was	c	had
4	a	didn't	b	isn't	c	wasn't
5	a	Before	b	After	c	Then
6	a	ski	b	skied	c	skiing
7	a	went	b	want	c	wait

6 How do you say these sentences in your language?

1 We went on a boat trip.

2 We had a great time.

3 He did it on his own.

4 I didn't stay for long.

5 They were in love.

6 He didn't care.

Extra reading

The garden-chair pilot

Before you read the newspaper article, look at the pictures of Larry Walters. Can you put the pictures in the right order?

Larry Walters, from San Pedro, California, lived his dream yesterday. His dream was to fly.

Larry bought 42 special weather-balloons and he filled them with helium. With the help of some friends, he attached the balloons to his garden chair. He had a bottle of soda, a radio and a camera. He also took a gun. Larry planned to shoot the balloons when he wanted to return to Earth.

His idea was to go up slowly but, in fact, his chair went up into the sky very quickly, and Larry lost his glasses. Soon he was at 3,500 metres. He stayed in the air for several hours and he began to feel cold and worried. At the end of the afternoon he was near Los Angeles International Airport. A plane went past him. The pilot closed his eyes and opened them again. It was true! There was a man in a garden chair in the clouds.

The wind started to take Larry over the sea, so he shot some of the balloons. But then he dropped his gun. His chair came down slowly, and he finally landed in a garden in Long Beach.

Larry said afterwards, 'I had the idea when I was thirteen years old. My dream came true. But I don't want to do it again!'

ABOUT FLYING

The first person to fly in a plane was Orville Wright in 1903. The plane was called Flyer 1 and the flight lasted for 12 seconds!

Task

1 Look at the article again and find 21 different verbs in the past simple. Make a list.
2 Look at the pictures and your list of verbs. Can you retell some of the story?

Unit 3   35

4 Entertainment

In Step 1 you study
- past simple: questions with *What ... ? Which ... ? How ... ?* etc.

so that you can
- ask for and give information about the past
- make a quiz about the past

Entertainment in the 20th century

2 Who were the Beatles?
- a *A basketball team.*
- b *A baseball team.*
- c *A pop group.*

1 Where was Bob Marley born?
- a *In Cuba.*
- b *In Jamaica.*
- c *In Kenya.*

3 What did John Logie Baird invent in 1925?
- a *The television.*
- b *The first computer.*
- c *The radio.*

1 Presentation *What did they do?*

a 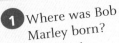 Listen to the quiz and follow in your book. Then check the words you don't understand.

b ⏱ Read the quiz and write the answers. If you don't know, guess. You've got five minutes! 1b

c Look at the answers below and check your score.

2 Key grammar *Past simple: questions*

Complete the questions with *was*, *were* and *did*.

Who	··········	John Logie Baird?
	··········	the Beatles?
What		Baird invent?
Where	··········	the first World Cup take place?

G ▸ 3b

3 Practice

a Make complete sentences.

1 Where did the Beatles come from?
2 Who were the Wailers?

1 Where / the Beatles come from ?
2 Who / the Wailers ?
3 Where / Bob Marley come from ?
4 What / the names of the four Beatles ?
5 When / the first World Cup take place ?
6 Why / Hollywood become famous ?
7 Who / J. R. R. Tolkien ?
8 How / Spiderman know that his friends were in danger ?
9 Which famous books / J. K. Rowling write ?

b How many questions can you answer?

c **Test a friend** Make another sentence for 3a. Can your friend complete the question?

Where / you buy those jeans?

Ask and answer the questions.

Answers

| 1 b | 2 c | 3 a | 4 b |
| 5 b | 6 b | 7 c | 8 a |

4 When did shops start to sell CDs?
  a In 1972.
  b In 1982.
  c In 1992.

7 How did Spiderman get his special powers?
  a He found a magic ring.
  b He was from the planet Krypton.
  c A radioactive spider bit him.

5 Where did the first World Cup Final take place?
  a In Argentina.
  b In Uruguay.
  c In Brazil.

8 Which famous book did J. R. R. Tolkien write?
  a The Lord of the Rings.
  b Lord of the Flies.
  c Solomon's Ring.

6 Why did the first film directors go to Hollywood?
  a Because a lot of film stars lived there.
  b Because they liked the weather and the landscape.
  c Because it was a famous place.

Writing and speaking

a Write questions in the past simple for these answers.

1 *What did you do at the weekend?*

1 I stayed at home.
2 A hot chocolate and some cereal.
3 At half past two.
4 I walked.
5 Yesterday.
6 At the market.

b Work with a friend. Ask and answer at least two of your questions. Give true answers.

Listening *Questions about you*

a 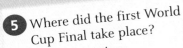 Listen to the questions. Are they about:

  a your school   b your meals   c your morning?

b 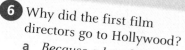 Listen again and write your answers.

1 *At quarter past seven.*

c Use your answers and make at least three sentences about your morning.

I got up at quarter past seven this morning.

Speaking *A class quiz*

Use what you know

Write at least one question about a famous person. Then work with your friends and ask and answer your questions.

Where was Nelson Mandela born?
What did Vincent Van Gogh paint?

> **Try this!**
> Write the names of an English or American book, film, writer, film star, pop group and footballer.

In Step 2 you study
● past simple: questions and short answers
● names of jobs

so that you can
● ask and answer questions about the past
● write an interview about a star's career

1 Presentation
Did you meet the stars?

a **What can you say about the photos?**

b 🔊 **Close your book and listen to the interview with Clare Burgess. What does she want to be?**

Clare Burgess works in the film industry. We asked her about her career.

INTERVIEWER: 1 ....

CLARE: Yes, I did. When I was 11, I decided I wanted to be a film director!

INTERVIEWER: 2 ....

CLARE: I studied media production at university. Then I got a job in a film studio.

INTERVIEWER: 3 ....

CLARE: No, I didn't! I helped the manager, I was his assistant.

INTERVIEWER: 4 ....

CLARE: Yes, it was. I learnt a lot. After that, I got a job with the Jim Henson Company. I worked in the computer animation section.

INTERVIEWER: You were lucky!

CLARE: Yes, I was very lucky, because then I went to New Zealand and worked on *The Lord of the Rings*.

INTERVIEWER: 5 ....

CLARE: No, I didn't, but I watched the filming sometimes. It was really exciting.

INTERVIEWER: 6 ....

CLARE: I still want to be a film director. But I need more experience.

INTERVIEWER: Well, good luck, Clare. And thanks for talking to us.

c **Read the interview and put the questions in the right place.**
1 c

a Did you meet all the stars?
b Was it interesting?
c Did you always want to work in the film industry?
d What did you do when you left school?
e So what do you want to do next?
f Did you direct any films?

🔊 **Listen again and check.**

2 Key grammar *Past simple: questions and short answers*

Complete the questions and answers.

.... it interesting?	Yes, it .... / No, it wasn't.
Were they famous?	Yes, they .... / No, they weren't.
.... you	help the manager? meet the stars?	Yes, I did. / No, I ....

Ⓖ▶ 2b. 4b

3 Practice

a Complete these questions.

1 <u>Did</u> Clare go to university?
2 .... she like her first job?
3 .... she happy in New Zealand?
4 .... she watch the filming?
5 .... the stars of the film talk to her?

b Now write the answers.

1 *Yes, she did.*

c Role play If you have time, work with a friend and imagine one of you is Clare. Ask and answer the questions in 3a.

> Did you go to university?

> Yes, I did.

4 Speaking

a Imagine you had an amazing weekend. Work with a friend and practise the conversation.

A: Did you have a good weekend?
B: Yes, I did. It was amazing.
A: What did you do?
B: I <u>went sky surfing in the Andes</u>.

b Change the <u>underlined</u> words and make another conversation. Here are some ideas.

I played football for ... .
I went to a party at ...'s house.
I had dinner with ... .

5 Key vocabulary *Jobs*

a Match the words with the pictures.

builder   waitress   farmer   shop assistant   secretary
mechanic   disc jockey   taxi driver

[🔊] Listen and check.

b Read the sentences and say who's speaking.

1 *The taxi driver.*

1 'I took Julia Roberts to her hotel yesterday.'
2 'I sold three DVD players and four TVs.'
3 'I finished the walls and started the floor.'
4 'I served Brad Pitt! He had a cheese omelette.'
5 'I worked on a Formula One racing car.'
6 'I went to the market and bought ten cows.'
7 'I organised a meeting and I wrote a report.'
8 'I played at a club in Tokyo last night.'

6 Writing and speaking *An interview*

Use what you know

Work with a friend and write a short interview with a real or an imaginary star.

A: Where did you go to school?
B: I went to school in Casablanca.
A: What was your first job?
B: I was a ...

Act your interview.

1 Key vocabulary
Past time expressions

a How do you say these time expressions in your language?

yesterday afternoon   in July
ten years ago   last night   last week
yesterday evening   this morning
two months ago   on Saturday   in 1989

b Put the time expressions in order. Start with *in 1989* and finish with *this morning*.

 Listen and check.

2 Reading   *Look at her now!*

Read the sentences and put the story in the right order. 1 d

a   It went into the charts two weeks ago.
b   Today she's everyone's favourite singer and her face is famous all over the world.
c   It was called *Last night*.
d   A year ago, she worked in a shop in Manchester and, once a month, she sang in a local club.
e   Last week it went to number one.
f   Then, three months ago, she appeared on a TV programme called *Tomorrow's Stars*.
g   A month ago, she made her first record.
h   Millions of people voted for her.

Listen and check your answers.

3 Writing and speaking

a **What about you?** Write true answers to these questions. When was the last time you:

1   went to the cinema? *Three weeks ago.*
2   did any sport?
3   listened to music?
4   bought a CD?
5   saw an interesting TV programme?
6   went to a football match?

b Work with a friend. Ask and answer at least two questions from 3a.

When was the last time you saw an interesting TV programme?

Last weekend. It was about the great white shark.

4 Listening   *Song*

a  Listen to the song *Last Night*. Who is the song about?

b Listen again. Find two time expressions. How many verbs in the past simple can you find?

5 Key pronunciation   /t/ /d/ /ɪd/

Listen and repeat the verbs.

1   /t/   walked cooked worked
2   /d/   closed answered served
3   /ɪd/   decided invented wanted

Now listen and put these verbs in the right group.

started   looked   stayed   voted   lived   talked

6 Writing   *A visit to the cinema*

Use what you know

Write at least four things about the last time you went to the cinema.

When did you go? Who did you go with?
What film did you see? Did you enjoy it?
Did your friend like the film? What did you do after the film?

If you prefer, choose one of the other things in Exercise 3.

Money or flowers?

The next morning Neesha and I got to school at 7.30, before everyone else.

'What are we looking for?' asked Neesha.

'I don't know,' I said. 'But let's go into the science room.'

We went in and looked around. There was nothing, just lots of notes about the wild flower project.

Suddenly the head came in.

'What are you doing?' asked Miss Kay.

'Just looking for our project notes,' I said.

'There isn't going to be a wild flower project now,' said Miss Kay. Then she took the notes out of our hands and left the room.

'Now what?' asked Neesha.

'I don't know,' I said. 'I can't think. I'm going for a walk.'

I walked onto the playing field opposite the school. That's where the wild flowers are, in a corner of the field. Mr Roberts says they're very important because they're really rare.

'I'm going to do the project,' I thought, 'even without Mr Roberts.'

Then I saw Miss Kay. She didn't see me. She was with her boyfriend. I knew him. He drove a big red car and bought and sold houses. He had a very loud voice. I could hear him easily.

'We can put twenty houses here,' he said. 'Maybe twenty-five.'

'Twenty-five houses is a lot of money,' said the head. She laughed. 'And the school gets the money from selling the playing field. Everyone wins.'

'Not everyone,' I thought. 'Not Mr Roberts.'

I knew now who put the exam paper into his desk and why.

Questions

1 Why did Tom and Neesha get to school early?
2 Why is the playing field important to Tom?
3 Why is the playing field important to Miss Kay and her boyfriend?

Extra exercises

1 Choose the right words.

1 Philip's family came to this town _____ 1998.
   a in
   b at
   c on

2 We went shopping _____ afternoon.
   a in
   b last
   c yesterday

3 What _____ do at university?
   a he did
   b did he
   c was he

4 Where did the last Olympic Games _____ place?
   a take
   b takes
   c took

5 _____ was the director of that film?
   a What
   b Who
   c Which

6 _____ time did we get home last night?
   a When
   b Which
   c What

2 Change the underlined words. Use time expressions with *ago*.

1 *three days ago*
1 Today is Monday. I met her on Friday.
2 It's 9.50 now. The train arrived at 9.30.
3 It's September now. I bought these jeans in September last year.
4 It's July now. We came here in February.
5 It's Saturday today. Donna left last Saturday.
6 Now it's 2006. Harry was born in 1993.
7 It's Wednesday today. They visited the museum last Thursday.
8 It's 8 o'clock now. The film started at 7 o'clock.

3 Write questions in the past simple.

1 *Was Elvis Presley a famous singer?*
1 Elvis Presley / a famous singer ?
2 Who / your favourite teacher last year ?
3 they / sell / a lot of records last month ?
4 Mel / sing / at the concert on Saturday ?
5 When / you / go / to New Zealand ?
6 Which film / Jack / see / last night ?

7 Why / you / put / my shoes in the cupboard ?
8 Joe and his band / on TV ?
9 Matt / run / to school this morning ?
10 How / you / do that ?

4 Complete the conversations.

1 Did you and Joe go out last Saturday?
   a To the cinema.
   b Yes, we did.
   c In the evening.

2 Who was your first English teacher?
   a Mr Johnson.
   b Four years ago.
   c He was very nice.

3 When did Sadie sell her bike?
   a At the market.
   b Last month.
   c Because she didn't like riding it.

4 Were Linda and Beth at the concert?
   a At the Tivoli Theatre.
   b At eight o'clock.
   c No, they weren't.

5 Which video did you watch?
   a Yes, I did.
   b We watched it after dinner.
   c *Titanic.*

5 Put the letters in the right order and write the names of the jobs. Then complete the sentences.

teswrasi   hiccmane   scid yokjec   hosp sinsatsta   remfra axit vredir

1 I want to buy this T-shirt. Where's the _____ ?
2 My grandfather is a _____ . He's got nearly a hundred cows.
3 Sarah's got a weekend job. She's a _____ at the Rose Café.
4 If you've got a problem with your car, go to Robert Jones. He's a very good _____ .
5 A _____ took us home from the station.
6 I don't want to dance. I don't think this _____ plays very good records.

6 How do you say these sentences in your language?

1 You were lucky!
2 It was really exciting.
3 Good luck!
4 Thanks for talking to us.
5 The song went into the charts.
6 It went to number one.

Life and culture

Making movies

Do you often go to the cinema?
What sort of films do you like?

In 1895 the Lumière brothers showed the first public film in a café in Paris. But it was Hollywood that became the centre of the film industry. In 1919, 35,000 people lived in Hollywood. In 1925, the population was 130,000.

The first 'talking movie', *The Jazz Singer*, appeared in 1927, and the first colour films appeared in the 1930s.

Today's films often use a mixture of real images and images from a computer. *Toy Story* was the first film made completely by computers, in 1995. It took 800,000 hours to create the pictures that you see on the screen.

The Lord of the Rings films took several years to make, and the actors used 1,600 pairs of 'hobbit' ears and feet! For the film *Harry Potter and the Philosopher's Stone*, the animal trainer Paul Wray worked for nine months with the owl Hedwig. For *Treasure Planet*, the art director Andy Gaskill created 11,000 different images – and the director only used 300 of them.

If you want to work in the film industry today, you need to have a lot of patience!

ABOUT THE FILM INDUSTRY

When the director George Lucas wanted to make *Star Wars*, the film company 20th Century Fox didn't like the idea. They didn't want to give him the money. But they changed their minds and the film made millions of dollars.

Task

Read the text and find the following things.

1 At least two important dates in the film industry.
2 The centre of the film industry.
3 A film that hasn't got any real people in it.
4 The name of a film with an owl in it.
5 Four jobs in the film industry.

Language summary

1 Dates

1st April 2005
2nd December 2009
23rd September 1998
4th August 1204
10th July 1873
19th February 2001

Check that you can

1.1 ● say dates in English.
Say the dates in the list.

> The first of April two thousand and five.

1.2 ● write dates in English.
Write these dates.

1 1st January 1963.

1 The first of January nineteen sixty-three.
2 The thirtieth of March nineteen eighty-four.
3 The eleventh of May two thousand and ten.
4 The fifteenth of October eighteen o two.
5 The twenty-ninth of June nineteen ninety-seven.
6 The third of November two thousand and five.

2 Past simple: *was/were*

Affirmative and negative

I/He/She/It	was wasn't	late yesterday.
We/You/They	were weren't	

Questions and answers

Was	I/he/she/it	late?
Were	we/you/they	
Yes, No,	I/he/she/it	was. wasn't.
Yes, No,	we/you/they	were. weren't.
wasn't = was not weren't = were not		

Check that you can

2.1 ● talk about the past with the correct form of *be*.
Complete the sentences with *was/wasn't, were/weren't*.

1 Marilyn Monroe _____ a famous film star.
2 I phoned you last night but you _____ there.
3 Matt _____ at school yesterday because he _____ ill.
4 Frodo and Sam _____ in *Star Wars*. They _____ in *The Lord of the Rings*.
5 When I _____ little, I _____ scared of dogs. I hated them.
6 Apollo 11 _____ an American spaceship. It _____ Russian.

2.2 ● ask questions with *Was/Were*.
Make a question and answer for each sentence.

1 Was it good? Yes, it was.

1 I saw *Treasure Planet* last night. (*good/yes*)
2 I bought some shoes yesterday. (*expensive/yes*)
3 We had an English test yesterday. (*difficult/no*)
4 I had an omelette for lunch. (*nice/yes*)
5 I got nine emails yesterday. (*interesting/no*)

3 Past simple: *regular and irregular verbs*

Regular verbs end in -*ed*. But a lot of verbs have an irregular past.

Affirmative

I	sailed to America.
You	travelled all over the world.
He/She/It	agreed with Ben.
We	slept in a tent.
You	went to New Zealand.
They	got up late.

See Spelling notes, page 143. Irregular verbs, page 142.

We form the negative of regular and irregular verbs with *didn't* + verb.

Negative

I		sail to America.
You		travel all over the world.
He/She/It	didn't	agree with Ben.
We		sleep in a tent.
You		go to New Zealand.
They		get up late.

We form questions in the past simple with *did* + verb.

Questions and answers

Did	you/he/she/it/they	sail to America? travel all over the world? agree with Ben? sleep in a tent? go to New Zealand? get up late?
Yes, No,	I/he/she/it/we/they	did. didn't.

Check that you can

3.1 ● describe events in the past.

Write sentences about yesterday.

1 She got up late yesterday.

1   Lisa always gets up late.
2   Ben always has sandwiches for lunch.
3   Lee usually walks to school.
4   Joe often plays his keyboard.
5   It often rains in Exeter.
6   Mrs Kelly usually goes to bed at ten.
7   Jack sees Ben every day.
8   Monica usually runs to work.
9   We usually leave the house at eight o'clock.
10 Mike usually arrives at work at nine.

Check that you can

3.2 ● describe things that didn't happen.

Complete the sentences with a verb in the negative.

1   We **had** English yesterday but we <u>didn't have</u> chemistry.
2   I **saw** Joe this morning but I _____ Ben.
3   Jack **came** last week but he _____ yesterday.
4   Sally **worked** on Saturday but she _____ on Sunday.
5   The Kellys **went** to Spain but they _____ to Madrid.
6   They **liked** the beach but they _____ the campsite.
7   I **enjoyed** the book but I _____ the film.
8   Sadie **took** her anorak but she _____ an umbrella.
9   The hotel manager **spoke** English but he _____ Italian.
10 We **ate** the chips but we _____ the salad.

Check that you can

3.3 ● ask and answer questions about the past.

Make questions with these verbs, then ask and answer.

invent   write   live   want   go   shoot   enjoy   have

> Did Alexander Bell invent the telephone?

> Yes, he did.

1   Alexander Bell / the telephone ?
2   Clare / to be a film star ?
3   the Romans / in England ?
4   Paul McCartney / the song *Angels* ?
5   Matt and Jack / to France on holiday ?
6   they / a good time ?
7   Billy / the sheriff ?
8   you / doing this exercise ?

4 Question words

> **What** did you do yesterday?
> **What** colour are your eyes?
> **When** did John Lennon die?
> **Where** are the Atlas mountains?
> **Who** was Diana Spencer?
> **Why** did you say that?
> **Which** jacket do you prefer?
> **How** do you make spaghetti bolognese?

Check that you can

● use the question words in the list.

Complete these sentences.

1   <u>When</u> did you go to bed last night?
2   _____ do you usually travel to school?
3   _____ is your brother in a bad mood?
4   _____ is your birthday?
5   _____ do you want for your birthday?
6   _____ train did they catch?
7   _____ is your favourite singer?
8   _____ does Mike Kelly live?
9   _____ time do you have your dinner?

5 Past simple + *ago*

They arrived It happened We saw Lisa	ten minutes three days two weeks a year	ago.

Check that you can

● say how long ago things happened.

Put the words in the right order and make sentences.

1 The match started ten minutes ago.

1   match / ago / ten / the / minutes / started
2   thirteen / Lisa / ago / years / born / was
3   died / Billy / long / a / ago / time
4   trainers / bought / I / six / ago / months / these
5   ago / came / ship / two / the / weeks
6   I / room / three / tidied / my / ago / days

Vocabulary

Holidays

beach
boat trip
campsite
caravan
ferry
hotel
ice cream
plane
rucksack
sea
sleeping bag
(to) stay at ...
tent

The wild west

dead
(to) die
horse
judge
(to) kill
prison
sheriff
(to) shoot
(to) steal

Jobs

builder
disc jockey
farmer
film director
manager
mechanic
secretary
shop assistant
taxi driver
waitress

Past time expressions

in 2004
in July
last night
last week
last month
last year
on Saturday
ten years ago
this morning
yesterday
yesterday morning
yesterday afternoon
yesterday evening

Expressions

Good luck!
He didn't care.
Thanks for talking to us.
They're in love.
We had a fantastic time.
You were lucky.

Study skills 2   Punctuation

Match the symbols with the words.

1 .   2 '   3 ?   4 !   5 ,   6 D

a question mark
b exclamation mark
c comma
d capital letter
e full stop
f apostrophe

🕐 Write these sentences again. Use the correct punctuation and capital letters. You've got four minutes!

1 can i use your rubber please
2 matt and his family live in manchester
3 hurry up
4 are you interested in athletics
5 yes i am
6 whats the time
7 ive got a sandwich an apple and a packet of crisps

See Spelling notes, page 143.

How's it going?

● Your rating

Look again at pages 44–45. For each section give yourself a star rating:

Good ☆ ☆ ☆   Not bad ☆ ☆   I can't remember much ☆

● Vocabulary

Choose five words from the Vocabulary list, then write a sentence with each word. Remember to check your punctuation.

● Test a friend

Look again at Units 3 and 4. Think of at least two questions, then ask a friend.

Why was Seb Clover famous?   What does 'farmer' mean?

● Correcting mistakes

Can you correct these mistakes?

1 I go to the cinema yesterday.
2 Where you go yesterday?
3 He runned across the road.

● Your Workbook

Complete the Learning Diaries for Units 3 and 4.

Coursework 2 **My window on the world**

Read Matt's newsletter, then write about famous people in your country. Use pictures and photos too.

Biographies

Hi! This month's newsletter is about some famous people in Britain and the USA.

Robin Hood

People believe that Robin Hood lived in England around 1300. There are many stories and films about him and his enemy, the Sheriff of Nottingham. Robin Hood was a hero and a villain. He stole money from the rich and he gave it to the poor.

Tiger Woods (1975–)

Tiger Woods is famous for his golf and also for his positive attitude. He became the world's number one player when he was only 21. In 1996 Tiger and his father Earl started the Tiger Woods Foundation. They wanted to motivate young people and help them to succeed.

J. K. Rowling (1965–)

Joanne Kathleen Rowling is the author of the Harry Potter books. She wrote her first story, called 'Rabbit', when she was six. Before she became famous, she worked as an English teacher. She had the idea for Harry Potter when she was on a train. It took five years to write the first book. Now you can buy her books in 200 different countries and read them in 61 languages.

Martin Luther King (1929–1968)

Martin Luther King was born in Atlanta, Georgia. He wanted equal rights for black people in the USA and he was the leader of the 'civil rights' campaign in the 1950s and 60s. He won the Nobel Peace Prize in 1964. An assassin killed King in Memphis when he was 39 years old.

Module 3

Out and about

In Module 3 you study

Grammar

- Present continuous
- Present simple and present continuous
- *There was/were; It was / They were*
- Past continuous
- *Could/couldn't*

Vocabulary

- Shops and things in a town
- Directions
- Places

so that you can

- Describe a journey across a town
- Understand and give directions
- Describe actions in progress at the moment
- Describe things that are generally true
- Describe a place in the past
- Talk about life in the past
- Talk about actions in progress in the past
- Write a short ghost story
- Talk about what was and wasn't possible in the past

Wild Flowers

Chapter 5 – Tom is in danger
Chapter 6 – Tom is a hero

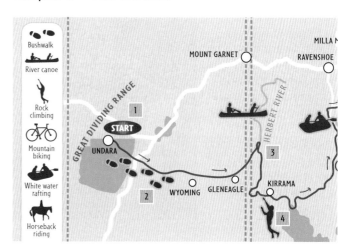

Life and culture

The Eco-Challenge Race
The first Americans

Coursework 3

A weekend in Manchester
You write about your town, or your capital city.

48

What's it about?

What can you say about the pictures?

Now match the pictures with sentences 1–5.

1 He walked across the park.
2 I was locking the door of the White Tower.
3 There was a church and a castle.
4 I could see smoke outside my room.
5 Lisa's spending the weekend in London.

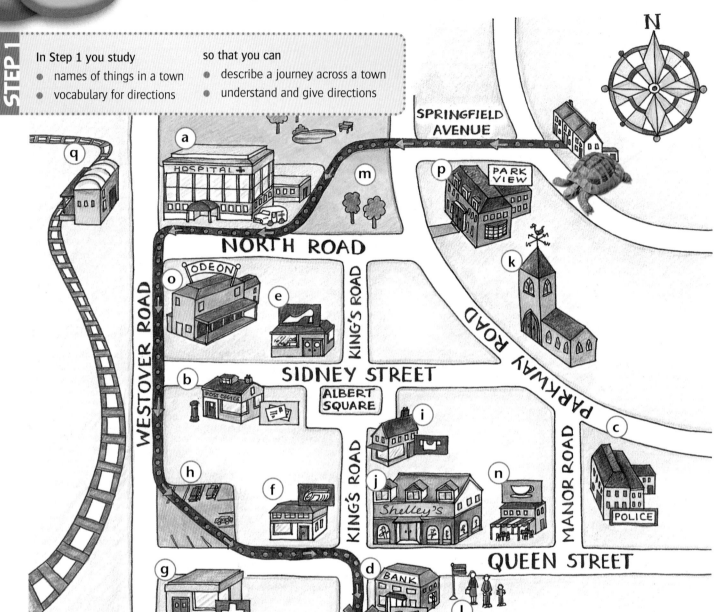

5 On the move

In Step 1 you study
- names of things in a town
- vocabulary for directions

so that you can
- describe a journey across a town
- understand and give directions

N

SPRINGFIELD AVENUE

PARK VIEW

NORTH ROAD

ODEON

KING'S ROAD

SIDNEY STREET

ALBERT SQUARE

WESTOVER ROAD

PARKWAY ROAD

MANOR ROAD

KING'S ROAD

Shelley's

POLICE

QUEEN STREET

BANK

1 Key vocabulary *In town*

a ⏱ Match these words with the letters on the map. You've got three minutes!

bank   car park   post office   police station
hospital   department store   shoe shop
clothes shop   chemist's   newsagent's

▭ Listen and check.

b Can you say the names of other places on the map?

2 Key pronunciation *Stress in words*

Put the words in the right group.

1 ● bank
2 ● ● car park
3 ● ● ● post office *hospital*
4 ● ● ● ● police station

▭ Listen and check.

Remember!

at the chemist's = at the chemist's shop.
at the newsagent's = at the newsagent's shop.

3 Reading and listening
He went across the park

a Read the notice and the newspaper article. Answer the questions.

  1 Who is Lightning?
  2 Where was he last weekend?
  3 Where is he now?

b 🔊 Listen to the newspaper article and follow Lightning's route on the map.

c Read the article again and write the words for numbers 1–10.

4 Key vocabulary
Directions

a How do you say these words in your language?

on the left   on the right
turn left   turn right
at the end of   go across
go along   go past

b Look at the map and complete the conversation with words from 4a.

Ben's standing outside the café. A woman's talking to him.

WOMAN: Excuse me, please. Can you tell me the way to the cinema?

BEN: Yes, sure. Go ¹_along_ Queen Street. Go ²_____ the department store, then ³_____ and go ⁴_____ King's Road. Go ⁵_____ Albert Square, then ⁶_____ and ⁷_____ Sidney Street. Turn ⁸_____ at the ⁹_____ of Sidney Street. The cinema is on the ¹⁰_____ .

WOMAN: Thanks very much.

🔊 Listen and check.

c **Role play** If you have time, work with a friend and practise the conversation.

LOST!

Our tortoise Lightning disappeared two days ago. If you see him, please contact:

Sadie Kelly
18 Maple Road
Tel. 01392 802465

A tortoise in town!

Tortoises aren't usually adventurous, but last Friday Lightning decided to spend the weekend in town. Several people saw Lightning on his amazing journey.

He left his home in Maple Road and went along Springfield Avenue. Then he

went across ¹_____ Road and walked across the ²_____ . He went past the ³_____ and then turned left at the end of the road. He went along ⁴_____ , past the ⁵_____ , and then he went across the ⁶_____ . He walked along ⁷_____ and then turned right.

Jill Martin, who works at the ⁸_____ opposite the car park, found Lightning outside the ⁹_____ on Monday morning. She took him to the ¹⁰_____ in Manor Road.

Lightning's owner, Sadie Kelly, said 'It was a shock when the police arrived, but it was great to see Lightning again!'

5 Listening *Can you tell me the way?*

🔊 Look at the map and imagine you're outside the café. Listen and follow the three sets of directions. Say where you are.

1 I'm outside the ...
2 I'm at the ...
3 I'm outside the ...

6 Speaking *Asking the way*

Use what you know

Work with a friend. Look at the map and imagine you're in Albert Square. Make at least one more conversation.

> Can you tell me the way to the post office ?

Or

> Yes, sure. Go along ...

If you prefer, talk about places near your school.

> Can you tell me the way to the library?

In Step 2 you study
- present continuous

so that you can
- describe actions in progress at the moment

1 Presentation *What are they doing?*

a **What can you say about the photos?**

Lisa's spending the weekend in London. She's at Paddington Station. Her cousin Finn's waiting for her, but she can't see him.

> Finn! Where are you?

> 1 .... clock near platform four. What are you doing?

> 2 .... you, of course! I'm at the end of platform nine.

> OK. Stay there. Don't move. 3 ....

> 4 .... T-shirt?

> Yes, I am.

> I can see you now!

> 5 ....

b **Complete the conversation between Lisa and Finn. Use these sentences.**

a Are you wearing a red ...
b I'm waiting for ...
c Hi, Lisa. Welcome to London.
d I'm standing under the ...
e I'm coming.

 Listen and check.

Try this!
What's the message?
IMWAITINGFORYOUOUTSIDETHESTAT
IONIMWEARINGABLACKCOATANDIMCARR
YINGAREDANDWHITEUMBRELLA

---

c **Complete the sentences with *Finn*, *Lisa* or *Finn and Lisa*.**

1 _Lisa_ 's waiting for her cousin, Finn.
2 .... are talking on their mobiles.
3 .... 's waiting for Lisa.
4 .... isn't standing under the clock.
5 .... are meeting at Paddington Station.
6 .... 's wearing a red T-shirt.

d **Role play** If you have time, act the conversation between Lisa and Finn.

2 Key grammar *Present continuous*

Complete the table.

I' _____ He's/She's They' _____	waiting for Lisa. talking.
I'm not He/She _____ They aren't	
Is he/she _____ you/they	coming?

G ➤ 5a–c

3 Practice

a Put the words in the right order and make sentences.

1 *Finn's standing under the clock.*

1 clock / standing / Finn's / the / under
2 on / talking / they're / mobiles / their
3 she / waiting / is ?
4 Lisa / what / and / Finn / doing / are ?
5 London / weekend / I'm / the / spending / in
6 isn't / anorak / wearing / she / an

b Test a friend Write another sentence for 3a. Can your friend say the right sentence?

lesson / having / English / an / we're

4 Reading and listening *Rap*

Read the rap. Can you guess the missing words?

Smiling

Hey! Hey! I'm not smiling.
I'm waiting for my friends.
I'm ¹_____ on the wall.
I'm ²_____ to hip-hop.
I'm not ³_____ I'm bored.
Just watching all the people while
    they're walking and they're ⁴_____ .
Hey! Hey! I'm not smiling.
She's ⁵_____ on the corner.
I don't ⁶_____ that I know her.
She's ⁷_____ cool cola.
Is she ⁸_____ for someone?
Hey! She's ⁹_____ at me.
Hey! She's ¹⁰_____ at me.
Hey! I'm smiling now. I'm smiling now.

🔲 Listen and check.

5 Listening and speaking
At Paddington Station

a 🔲 Listen to three conversations at Paddington Station. Match the conversations with the pictures.

b Work with a friend. Imagine you're one of the people in 5a. Use these verbs to describe what you're doing.

have   sit   wear   meet   carry   buy   go

Can your friend guess who you are?

> I'm drinking a glass of orange juice. I'm sitting in the café.

> I know! You're the woman in picture c.

6 Writing and speaking *On the phone*

Use what you know

Work with a friend. Imagine you're in town. You can't find your friend. Write a telephone conversation, then act your conversation.

A: Where are you?
B: I'm outside the shoe shop.
A: Who are you with?
B: I'm on my own.
A: What are you doing?
B: I'm waiting for you.

Add more things if you can.

In Step 3 you study
- present simple and present continuous

so that you can
- describe things that are generally true and actions in progress at the moment

1 Presentation
At the moment or every day?

a **What can you say about the picture?**

b **Close your book and listen to the description of Jono. Where's he going?**

Jono Grant lives in London. He works in the music industry. He writes dance music. He also works as a disc jockey. Two or three times a year, he goes to Japan. He plays his music at a club in Tokyo.

At the moment, he's on the tube – the underground railway in London. He's on his way to Heathrow Airport. He's going to Japan. He's looking at a music magazine but he's thinking about his girlfriend in Tokyo.

c **Are these sentences true, false or 'we don't know'?**

1 Jono doesn't live in Tokyo.
2 At the moment, he's going to the airport.
3 He reads a lot of music magazines.
4 At the moment, he's writing some music.
5 He's playing his music.
6 He often thinks about his girlfriend in Tokyo.
7 He flies to Japan two or three times a year.

2 Key grammar
Present continuous / present simple

Complete the explanation with *things that are generally true* and *actions in progress at the moment*.

> **Present simple**
> Jono goes to Tokyo two or three times a year.
>
> **Present continuous**
> He's going to Tokyo today.
>
> *We use the present simple for* _____
> *We use the present continuous for* _____

 1c, 5c

3 Practice

a **Choose the right tense and make complete sentences.**

1 The sun's shining.

It's twelve o'clock in London and the sun ¹_____ (*shine*). It's nine in the evening in Tokyo. Jono ²_____ (*sit*) in a restaurant with his girlfriend. They ³_____ (*eat*) sushi and they ⁴_____ (*talk*) about his new CD. Jono ⁵_____ (*not eat*) sushi very often but his girlfriend ⁶_____ (*love*) it.

b **Make two sentences for each person, one in the present simple and one in the present continuous.**

1 Karen works in a department store.
At the moment she's going home.

1 Karen is a shop assistant in a department store. At the moment she's on the tube.
2 Will has got a job in a bank. At the moment he's in the park on his skateboard.
3 Sue is a teacher. At the moment she's in her garden.
4 Dave is a footballer. At the moment he's at home in the kitchen.
5 Asha is a waitress. At the moment she's at the cinema.

4 Writing *An imaginary person*

Use what you know

Look at the picture of the people on the tube. Use your imagination and describe one of the people.

Where does he/she live? What does he/she do? Where's he/she going? What's he/she thinking about at the moment?

Tom is in danger

I ran back and told Neesha about the head and her boyfriend and the playing field.

'This is terrible,' she said. 'We must tell the police.'

'Yes,' I said. 'But we haven't got any proof. The police are going to believe the head.'

'I've got an idea,' said Neesha. 'My dad's got a really small tape recorder. He uses it for work. We can record what the head says.'

The head lived near Neesha, in a quiet road, near the park. That evening we went to her house. I walked up to the front door and Neesha waited by the garden wall. The head wasn't at home, but her horrible boyfriend was there.

'I was just talking to your cat about you, and now here you are,' he said when he saw me. And there, in the dining room, was Maggie. I ran towards her. The boyfriend followed me and then he locked the door behind us.

'You can't lock me in here,' I said. 'My friends are waiting for me.' I spoke loudly so that the tape recorder got every word.

'You can go home soon,' he said. 'But first Miss Kay wants to talk to you.'

'You took my cat,' I said. Maggie mewed. She looked hungry.

'Yes,' he replied.

'And you put the exam paper in Mr Roberts' desk,' I told him.

'I didn't,' he said. 'Your head teacher did that.' He laughed. He had a horrible laugh.

'I can tell the police about that and about the playing field,' I said.

'I don't think so, Tom,' he said. 'Because everyone believes a head teacher. And tomorrow Miss Kay's going to find something really bad in your school bag. After that, no one's going to believe a word you say.'

Then he went out and locked the door again.

Questions

1 Why didn't Tom and Neesha go to the police?
2 Why did they need a tape recorder?
3 Was the head's boyfriend worried?

Extra exercises

1 Choose the right words.

1 Sadie's _____ her computer at the moment.
   - a use
   - b uses
   - c using

2 Look at Jack. _____ new trainers.
   - a He wear
   - b He wears
   - c He's wearing

3 Barney and Lee are at home. They _____ football this afternoon.
   - a isn't playing
   - b aren't playing
   - c don't play

4 It's Sunday! _____ thinking about school today.
   - a I
   - b I'm not
   - c I don't

5 _____ Lisa smiling?
   - a Is
   - b Are
   - c Does

6 What _____ at the moment?
   - a do you read
   - b you're reading
   - c are you reading

2 Complete the sentences with words for places in town.

1 If someone steals your bag, go to the _____ station.
2 Leave your car in the _____ next to the supermarket.
3 _____ stores are very large shops. They sell lots of different things.
4 A _____ is a place for people when they're very ill.
5 A _____ sells newspapers and magazines.
6 You can buy dresses, trousers, sweaters and socks at a _____ shop.
7 Save your money and put it in the _____ .
8 You can send letters from a _____ office.

3 Complete the directions.

A: Can you tell me [1]_____ to the library, please?

B: Yes, sure. [2]_____ the square to the church and [3]_____ left. Go along Martin Street, [4]_____ the cinema, and then [5]_____ Smith Street. The library is [6]_____ .

A: Thanks very much.

- a Go across
- b turn
- c the way
- d on the right
- e past
- f go along

4 Complete the conversations.

1 Who are you writing to?
   - a My aunt in Australia.
   - b I never write letters.
   - c I like sending emails.

2 What do you do?
   - a I'm doing my homework.
   - b I'm a disc jockey.
   - c I'm going to bed.

3 What are you doing?
   - a I'm in the bath.
   - b I'm a mechanic.
   - c I study animals.

4 What sort of food do you eat?
   - a I'm eating chicken and salad.
   - b A banana.
   - c I like vegetarian food.

5 What are you reading?
   - a Magazines, usually.
   - b I read history books.
   - c A book about the Internet.

5 Complete the sentences. Use the present simple or the present continuous.

1 At the moment Joanne _____ on the platform. She _____ to work by train every morning. (stand / go)
2 Francisco _____ in the shop today. He never _____ on Sunday. (not work / work)
3 They often _____ cards after dinner, but this evening they _____ to music. (play / listen)
4 I _____ the video because I _____ horror films. (not watch / not like)
5 Karen always _____ home at 6.30. She _____ dinner now. (get / have)
6 Our cousins often _____ the weekend with us. They _____ with us this weekend. (spend / stay)

6 How do you say these sentences in your language?

1 Excuse me, please. Can you help me?
2 It was great to see him again.
3 Can you tell me the way to the library?
4 Welcome to London.
5 She works at the chemist's.
6 I'm on my way to the airport.

Extra reading

Life and culture

The Eco-Challenge Race

Do you know the names of any famous races?
Do you watch any of them on TV?

Bushwalk

River canoe

Rock climbing

Mountain biking

White water rafting

Horseback riding

Sea Kayak

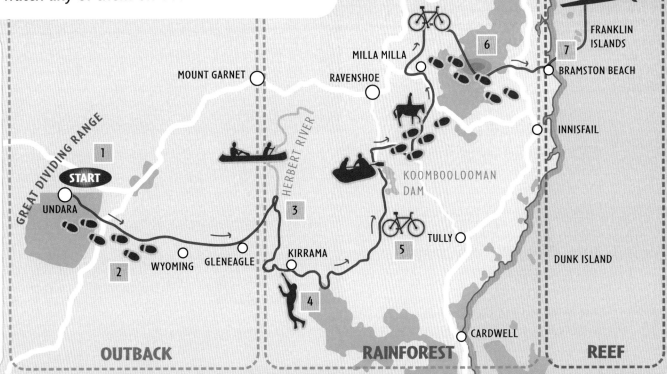

The Eco-Challenge Race takes place once a year, usually in a different country each year. There are four people in each team, and the teams come from all over the world. The race is about 500 kilometres long.

The competitors travel for six to 12 days, sometimes for 24 hours a day, so they don't get much sleep. They walk through rainforests. They ride horses across the desert. They travel across the sea. They go up mountains on mountain bikes. They go down rivers and across lakes.

The natural environment is very important in the Eco-Challenge. The teams must not put their tents on top of plants and they must not leave any rubbish. Before the race the competitors do something to help the local people. For example, in Morocco, they cleaned the beaches. In Fiji, they collected books for local schools. In the US, they worked in a children's park.

The race is always exciting and it is always very, very hard. When it took place in Canada, 70 teams started and only 14 finished.

ABOUT THE RACE

The Eco-Challenge adventure race started in 1995.
You can read more about it on the Internet.

Task

Look at the map of the race in Australia. Match these sentences with the numbers on the map.

a They climbed some rocks near Kirrama.

b They went past the Franklin Islands.

c They walked through the outback to the Herbert River.

d The race started here.

e They walked through the rainforest to the top of a mountain.

f The race finished here.

g They went across the sea in kayaks.

h They rode on mountain bikes.

i They went down the river in canoes.

In Step 1 you study
- names of places
- *There was/were; It was / They were*

so that you can
- describe a place in the past
- talk about life in the past

1 **Key vocabulary** *Places*

📻 Listen and say the words in the list, then find them in the pictures.

There's a forest in picture a.

church   town   castle   market
forest   skyscraper   river   factory
square   bridge   village
town hall

One thing isn't in the pictures – what is it?

2 **Presentation**

What was it like?

a 📻 Listen and follow the story of the town in your book. Is there a picture of the town today?

b Match these sentences with the pictures. Some sentences are true for several pictures.

   1 Pictures a and b.

   1 There wasn't a bridge across the river.
   2 There was a church.
   3 There wasn't a town hall.
   4 It was a busy town.
   5 It was very quiet.
   6 It was two hundred years ago.
   7 There weren't any big buildings.
   8 It was a small village.
   9 There were some shops.
   10 There weren't any streets.

10,000 BC

Twelve thousand years ago, our town wasn't a town. It was a camp for people of the Stone Age. The people were hunters. They lived in tents by the river. There was a forest round the camp.

2,000 BC

Four thousand years ago, our town was a small village. The people were farmers. There were some simple houses, but there weren't any streets.

110 AD

In the year 110, our town was a Roman town. There was a bridge across the river. There were several shops and there was a bar. There was a school too.

1200

The Roman town didn't survive and, in 1200, our town was a village again – a medieval village. There was a church and a castle. There was a shoe shop and a baker's. Once a week, there was a market.

1820

In 1820, it was a busy town again. There was a new church, a hotel, a town hall and a square. There were a lot of different shops and there was a big factory.

---

3 Key grammar *There was / It was*

a How do you say these sentences in your language?

> 1 There was a church. It was near the river.
> 2 There were two shops. They weren't very big.
>
> **G** ► 17c

b Complete the questions and answers.

> .... there a church? | Yes, there was.
> Was it near the river? | Yes, ... was.
> Were .... any shops? | Yes, there ....
> .... they very big? | No, ... weren't.

4 Practice

a Complete the answers with *there*, *it* or *they*.

1 Was there a factory? Yes, *there was* .
2 Was it very noisy? Yes, ...
3 Were there any animals? Yes, ...
4 Were they near the houses? Yes, ...
5 Were the Romans English? No, ...
6 Was the castle in the forest? No, ...

b Test a friend Think of a true/false sentence about one of the pictures.

In 1820, there weren't any shops.   (False.)

5 Listening and speaking *Sounds from the past*

a 🔊 Listen to the sounds and match them with the pictures.

b 🔊 Listen again. Say what you heard for each picture.

(There was a clock.)   (There were sheep.)

6 Speaking

Imagine you were a teenager in the 13th century. Work with a friend and complete the conversation.

A: Were you and your family rich?
B: ....
A: What was your house like?
B: ....
A: Was there a school in your village?
B: ....
A: Were there any shops?
B: ....

7 Speaking and writing *Your town*

Use what you know

Imagine your town or village two hundred years ago. What was it like? Share your ideas, then write at least four sentences.

It was quite small. There weren't any big shops.

In Step 2 you study
- past continuous

so that you can
- talk about actions in progress in the past
- write a short ghost story

1 Reading *At the Tower*

a Look at the pictures and read the text. Who was Anne Boleyn?

> Many years ago, the Tower of London was a prison. King Henry VIII sent two of his six wives there. Anne Boleyn, his second wife, was executed on Tower Green in 1536.

b Match pictures 1–3 with these descriptions.

a The ghost is walking through the wall.

b The guard is standing at the bottom of the steps. He's locking the door.

c There's a woman at the top of the steps. She's crying. She's wearing a long grey dress.

2 Presentation *Was he dreaming?*

a 🔊 Cover the text, look at the pictures and listen to the conversation. Did Finn and Lisa see a ghost at the Tower?

Lisa and Finn are visiting the Tower of London. They're talking to one of the guards.

LISA: Are there any ghosts here?

GUARD: Oh yes! A couple of years ago, I saw the ghost of Anne Boleyn.

LISA: Did you really? Tell us about it!

GUARD: It was six o'clock and it was getting dark. Suddenly, I saw a strange light. There was a woman at the top of the steps.

FINN: It was probably a visitor.

GUARD: No, it wasn't a visitor. She was wearing a long, grey dress and her face was very pale. She was crying.

LISA: Where were you?

GUARD: I was standing at the bottom of the steps. I was locking the door of the White Tower, but I dropped my keys!

FINN: Perhaps you were dreaming.

GUARD: No, I wasn't dreaming. It was real, I'm sure of that.

FINN: But how can you be sure it was a ghost?

GUARD: Because she came down the steps and then she walked through the wall and disappeared!

> **Try this!** Find the names of three places in London.
>
> BTIHGEBTEONWBEURCOKFILNOGNHDAOMNPALACE

b 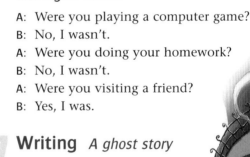 **Listen again and follow in your book. Are these sentences true or false? Correct the false sentences.**

1 The guard saw the ghost two years ago.
2 It was six o'clock in the morning.
3 He was locking the door when he saw a woman.
4 It was a visitor.
5 The woman was standing at the bottom of the steps.
6 She wasn't wearing modern clothes.
7 She wasn't happy.
8 The guard dropped his keys.
9 It wasn't real. The guard was dreaming.
10 The ghost opened the door.

3 Key grammar
Past continuous

Complete the explanation.

I/He/She	was wasn't	
		crying.
We/You/They	were weren't	
Was I/he/she Were we/you/they	dreaming?	

Yes, I was. / No, I wasn't.
Yes, we were. / No, we weren't.

We form the past continuous with _____ or _____ and a verb + _____ . We use it for actions in progress in the past.

G→ 6a-d

4 Practice

Complete the story. Make sentences in the past continuous.

1 *Anne Boleyn was sitting in her room.*

It was eleven o'clock in the morning on 19th May 1536. Anne Boleyn ¹_____ (*sit*) in her room in the White Tower. She ²_____ (*wear*) a long grey dress and she ³_____ (*write*) her final words before her execution. At Greenwich Palace, King Henry ⁴_____ (*talk*) to his future wife, Jane Seymour. He ⁵_____ (*not think*) about Anne. At twelve o'clock, Anne was dead. Henry and Jane ⁶_____ (*walk*) through the palace garden. They ⁷_____ (*laugh*). The birds ⁸_____ (*sing*) and the sun ⁹_____ (*shine*). At the Tower, the guards ¹⁰_____ (*carry*) Anne's body to St Peter's Chapel and the air was silent and cold.

5 Key pronunciation *Intonation in questions*

 Listen and repeat the sentences. Do they go up or down?

1 What were they doing?
2 Were they laughing?
3 What was she doing?
4 Was she crying?

6 Speaking

What about you? Work with a friend. What was your friend doing at seven o'clock last night? Guess.

A: Were you playing a computer game?
B: No, I wasn't.
A: Were you doing your homework?
B: No, I wasn't.
A: Were you visiting a friend?
B: Yes, I was.

7 Writing *A ghost story*

Use what you know

Write a short ghost story. Answer these questions.

What was the time?
Where were you?
What were you doing?
What did you see?
What was the ghost like?
Were you scared?
What was the ghost doing when you saw it?
Then what happened?

In Step 3 you study
- *could/couldn't*

so that you can
- talk about what was and wasn't possible in the past

1
I woke up suddenly. My sister was asleep. I could hear my mother's voice. She was shouting 'Quick! Get up!' I could see smoke outside my room.

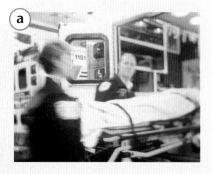

1 Presentation
I couldn't move my arm

a ⏱ Match the photos with the stories. You've got two minutes!

Ben, Mel and Jack remember three bad days.

2
I was skateboarding in the park when I fell. Everything went black. When I woke up, I didn't know where I was. I couldn't move my arm.

a

b

3
I woke up at half past five. It was getting light so I got up. I went into the kitchen and made some breakfast, but I couldn't eat it.

c

b Now choose the right sentence and finish each story.

a It was broken and I was in hospital.
b Our house was on fire.
c It was the first day of our exams.

c 📻 Listen and check your answers.

2 Key grammar *could/couldn't*

Complete the explanation.

I / You He/She We/ They	could couldn't	hear a voice. move.

Could *and* couldn't *are the past tense of* _____ *and* _____ .

Ⓖ➤ 11c

3 Practice

Complete the sentences with *could* or *couldn't*.

1 Ben was in hospital. He **couldn't** move his arm.
2 After the fire, Mel _____ go back to her house, so she went to a friend's house.
3 When Ben woke up, he _____ hear a voice. It was the nurse.
4 Jack's exams weren't too bad. He _____ answer nearly all the questions.
5 After his accident, Ben _____ go skateboarding for a long time.
6 Jack got up early because he _____ sleep.

4 Speaking and writing *Ben's broken arm*

Use what you know

When Ben broke his arm, life wasn't easy. Think of things he couldn't do and things he could do. Make a list and then share your ideas.

He couldn't get dressed on his own, but he could clean his teeth.

Tom is a hero

What could I do? I was locked in a dining room with my cat. I could open the window a bit, but only a few centimetres. There was a lock to stop it opening. I called, and Neesha heard me.

'I've got it,' I said. 'But I can't get out!' I threw out the tape recorder. Neesha caught it.

'Take it to the police quickly,' I said to her.

'Are you OK?' she asked.

'Just go,' I shouted.

She turned and ran down the road.

Time went really slowly. Maybe the tape recorder didn't work, I thought. Maybe the head was on her way home. I counted the minutes. Twenty minutes passed. At last a police car arrived.

'Help!' I called.

'OK, OK, don't be scared, we're here,' a policeman shouted.

The policeman came into the house and unlocked the dining room door.

'I couldn't get out,' I said.

'It was just a joke,' said the head's boyfriend.

'Really?' asked the policeman. He played the tape and the boyfriend went very white.

'You and Miss Kay are in a lot of trouble,' said the policeman.

The next day, Mr Roberts came back to school. For once everyone wanted to hear my story and they didn't want any jokes. Then Mr Roberts gave me a present – a microscope.

After that, they wrote about my story in the newspapers. And they took pictures of Neesha and me next to the flowers. Mr Roberts was right. The flowers were really special.

In the end, I decided, school wasn't really boring at all.

Questions

1 Why couldn't Tom get out of Miss Kay's house?
2 What did Neesha do?
3 What happened when the police arrived?
4 Was everyone interested in Tom's story? Did you enjoy it?

Extra exercises

1 Choose the right words.

1 We couldn't _____ here on time because the bus was late.
   a get
   b got
   c to get

2 Sixty years ago _____ wasn't a supermarket in our town.
   a there
   b it
   c they

3 A: Were there any good films on TV?
   B: Yes, _____ .
   a they did
   b they were
   c there were

4 Adam _____ ride a horse when he was five years old.
   a did
   b was
   c could

5 Lisa waved to her friends. _____ standing at the top of the stairs.
   a They're
   b They were
   c There were

6 When I saw Kim, _____ along South Street.
   a she's walking
   b she walked
   c she was walking

2 Are these sentences true or false?

1 You use a bridge to go across a river.
2 Lots of people go shopping in factories.
3 Towers are usually quite tall.
4 People buy and sell things at a market.
5 You often find skyscrapers in a village.
6 People didn't live in castles.
7 There are hundreds of trees in a forest.
8 You buy fruit and vegetables at the baker's.

3 Complete the sentences. Use *there was/were/wasn't/weren't*.

1 Inside the castle _____ about thirty rooms.
2 _____ an interesting programme on the radio yesterday.
3 _____ any boats on the lake yesterday. It was very cold and windy.
4 _____ some money on my desk this morning, but it isn't here now.
5 We couldn't dance because _____ any music at the party.
6 _____ some new computer magazines at the newsagent's.

4 Complete the sentences. Use the past continuous form of the verbs.

1 At 5.30 yesterday afternoon Paul _____ for his science exam. (*study*)
2 Julie and Sam _____ in the café when we came in. (*sit*)
3 I was cold because I _____ a jacket. (*not wear*)
4 The sun _____ when we left home this morning. (*not shine*)
5 My parents _____ ready when the taxi arrived. (*get*)
6 You _____ the computer, so I decided to surf the Internet. (*not use*)

5 Complete the questions with *was* or *were*. Then match them with the answers.

1 What _____ the restaurant like?
2 What _____ you doing?
3 _____ there a telephone in the flat?
4 _____ you visiting your grandparents?
5 _____ the town hall open?
6 _____ there any people in the room?

a No, there wasn't.
b No, it was closed.
c Yes, there were about twenty.
d I was reading in my room.
e It was OK but it was a bit noisy.
f No, I was shopping in town.

6 How do you say these sentences in your language?

1 What was your house like?
2 I saw a ghost. – Did you really?
3 I met him a couple of years ago.
4 I'm sure of that.
5 Quick! Get up!
6 It's getting light.

The first Americans

What do you know about the history of the USA? Do you know who Crazy Horse was?

Thirty thousand years ago the first Americans travelled across the ice from Asia to Alaska. Some of them stayed in Alaska and became the Inuit people. Others went to different parts of Canada and North and South America. Some were fishermen, some were farmers and some were hunters. When Columbus arrived in the Caribbean in 1492, he thought he was in India, so he called the Native Americans 'Indians'.

When the first Europeans went to live in North America, there were already a million people there. There were about 300 'Indian' tribes. Each tribe had a different language and way of life, but they also had a sign language that everyone could understand.

When the first white settlers* arrived, the Native Americans were living in their traditional homes across North America. At first, they were friendly to their new neighbours, but the European settlers wanted their land. The 'Indians' fought many wars and their leaders – Crazy Horse, Geronimo, Sitting Bull – became famous. Thousands of them died, and they also died from illnesses that the Europeans brought with them. Finally, the US government forced the Native Americans to live in special 'reservations'.

Today, about 1.5 million Native Americans live on reservations. Many of them try to keep their ancient traditions and now Native American culture is growing again.

* European immigrants

ABOUT NATIVE AMERICAN CULTURE

Did you know that hot chocolate, popcorn and chewing gum come from the Native Americans?

Task

Read the text, then look at these sentences. Are they true or false? Correct the false sentences.
1 The first Americans arrived there in 1300.
2 The first Native Americans came from Asia.
3 When the Europeans arrived, there were 300 Native Americans.
4 The settlers called them Indians because they lived in India.
5 The Native Americans and the Europeans didn't fight at first.
6 The Native Americans didn't want to lose their traditional homes.
7 Crazy Horse was one of their leaders.
8 The members of the US government lived in 'reservations'.
9 Today no one is interested in Native American culture.

Language summary

1 Present continuous

Affirmative

I'm He's/She's/It's We're/You're/They're	making a noise.

Negative

I'm not He/She/It isn't We/You/They aren't	listening.

Questions and answers

Am I Is he/she Are we/you/they	going the right way?

Yes, I am.   No, I'm not.   Yes, he/she is.   No, he/she isn't.   Yes, we/you/they are.   No, we/you/they aren't.
We can say he isn't *or* he's not.   *We can say* they aren't *or* they're not.

Check that you can

* describe what's happening around you at the moment. Write true answers to these questions.

1 What are you wearing today?
2 Where are you sitting at the moment?
3 Are you sitting by a window?
4 Is it raining outside?
5 Are you writing with a pen or a pencil?

2 Present continuous and present simple

There are two present tenses in English.
The present continuous describes 'temporary' actions – things 'in progress' at the moment:
You're reading about the present continuous.
Lisa's visiting her cousin in London.
The present simple describes things that are generally true:
Tortoises don't move very fast.
and habits and routines:
Sue gets up at seven and she has a shower.

Check that you can

* use the two different present tenses.

Write complete sentences. Use the present simple or present continuous.

1 *It's half past six and Danny's getting up. He always gets up at half past six.*

1 It's half past six and Danny _____ . He always _____ at half past six. (*get up/get up*)
2 It's half past seven and Mike _____ at the bus stop. He _____ for the 88 bus. (*stand/wait*)
3 Sue can't answer the phone because she _____ her hair. She _____ it three times a week. (*wash/wash*)
4 Sally always _____ to her Spanish cassette in the car. She's _____ the past tense at the moment. (*listen/learn*)

See Spelling notes, page 143.

3 Past continuous

Affirmative and negative

I/He/She/It	was wasn't	running very fast.
We/You/They	were weren't	

Questions and answers

Was he/she	waiting for the bus?
Were you/they	

Yes, No,	I/he/she	was. wasn't.
Yes, No,	we/you/they	were. weren't.

Check that you can

3.1 * describe actions in progress in the past.

Write sentences with the past continuous.

1 *Sue and Mike were driving home.*

1 At half past nine last night, Sue and Mike _____ home. (*drive*)
2 There were two badgers in our tent. They _____ our food. (*eat*)
3 It was quarter to seven. It _____ dark. (*get*)
4 Tom was scared. Someone _____ him. (*follow*)
5 There was smoke in the kitchen. My toast _____ . (*burn*)
6 I didn't hear the phone because I _____ a bath. (*have*)

3.2 • ask questions with the past continuous.
Make questions, then ask and answer.

> Was Lara sitting in a café?

> Yes, she was.

1 Lara / sit in a café ? (*Yes*)
2 Mike / walk across the square ? (*No*)
3 Tom and Shona / listen to music ? (*No*)
4 Val and Eric / play cards ? (*Yes*)

4 Past continuous and past simple

We use the past continuous for actions in progress in the past:
It was four o'clock in the morning. I was dreaming about David Beckham.

and the past simple for 'completed' actions:
Suddenly, our dog jumped onto my bed.

| I was walking home
He was driving to work
We were talking	when	a lion ran across the road.

Check that you can

• use these two different past tenses.

Put the verbs into the past simple or the past continuous.

> 1 *When Lee arrived at school, his friends were playing football outside.*

1 When Lee .... at school, his friends .... football outside. (*arrive/play*)
2 Ben .... when he .... his arm. (*skateboard/break*)
3 My gran .... down the steps when she .... (*walk/fall*)
4 When Ben .... , a nurse .... by the bed. (*wake up/stand*)
5 The guard .... the gate when he .... his keys. (*lock/drop*)
6 My friend and I .... for the bus when we .... Lee. (*wait/see*)

5 There/It/They

There's a scorpion under my bed. It's enormous.

There were fifty people at my party and they were all very noisy.

Check that you can

• use *There* and *It/They.*

Complete these sentences.

1 .... 's a bus at the bus stop. .... 's a number 32.
2 .... were three emails, but .... were all from Lisa.
3 .... are some keys on the table. Are .... Sue's?
4 When I woke up, ... was a bat in my room. .... was on the wardrobe.

6 could, couldn't

The past tense of *can/can't* is *could/couldn't.*

> I couldn't read well when I was at primary school.
> It was great. We could go swimming and riding.
> Could Ben move his arm?
> Yes, he could. / No, he couldn't.

Check that you can

• describe things that were or weren't possible.

Complete the sentences with *could* or *couldn't.*

1 Jack wasn't hungry and he .... eat anything.
2 Zoe's amazing. She .... speak Italian, Spanish and English when she was four.
3 It was getting light and I .... see the trees outside my window.
4 We .... get a video because the shop was closed.

7 Verbs and prepositions

We often use verbs of movement (*go, walk, sail*) with a preposition (*across, past, down*).

Go
We went
often walk	**across** the square.
along King's Road.
past the park.
through the wood.
down the steps.
up the hill.

Check that you can

• describe people's 'movements'.

Which sentences make sense? Which sentences don't make sense? Write *Yes* or *No* for each sentence.

1 We often walk along the chemist's. *No.*
2 He ran past Africa and stopped outside the bank.
3 He ran across Africa. It was an amazing journey.
4 Seb sailed down the river to the sea.
5 I often walk along the river and through the wood.

Vocabulary

Places

bridge
forest
hill
river

town
village

bank
building
café
car park
castle
church
cinema
factory
hospital
market
park
police station
post office
road
shop
skyscraper
square
station
street
town hall

Shops

baker's
chemist's
clothes shop
department store
newsagent's
shoe shop

Directions

at the end of
(to) go across
(to) go along
(to) go past
on the left
on the right
(to) turn left
(to) turn right

Expressions

a couple of years
Can you tell me
    the way?
Did you really?
It was great to see
    him/her.
Welcome to London!
Yes, sure.

Study skills 3 Remembering vocabulary

Here are six ways to remember new vocabulary.
🕐 Match the pictures with the sentences. You've got four minutes!

1 Make groups of words for different topics.
2 Write some new words and put them on your bedroom wall.
3 Use pictures, or write the word in your language.
4 Invent sentences with new words.
5 Underline the stress in words with more than one syllable.
6 Think about vocabulary when you're on the bus.

How many of these things do you do?

How's it going?

- ### Your rating

Look again at pages 66–67. For each section give yourself a star rating:
Good ☆ ☆ ☆   Not bad ☆ ☆   I can't remember much ☆

- ### Vocabulary

Choose six words from the Vocabulary list and do at least three of the things in Study skills.

- ### Test a friend

Look again at Units 5 and 6. Think of at least two questions, then ask a friend:

> How do you ask for directions in English?
> Who did Finn and Lisa talk to?

- ### Correcting mistakes

Can you correct these mistakes?

1 ~~I go now. Do you come?~~
2 ~~There was four boys in my grandfather's family.~~
3 ~~Were you dreaming? Yes, I were.~~

- ### Your Workbook

Complete the Learning Diaries for Units 5 and 6.

Coursework 3   My window on the world

Read Matt's newsletter, then write about your town, or your capital city. Use pictures, maps and photos too.

A weekend in Manchester

Hi! This month's newsletter is about my home city, Manchester.

You can get the metro shuttle to the shops and the city centre. It's free and it goes every ten minutes.

The shops usually open at nine and close at six, sometimes later. Some of the shops are open on Sunday too. I don't know why, but people in Britain love going shopping!

At the Salford Watersports Centre you can have lessons in canoeing and windsurfing.

If you're a football fan, then the Manchester United Tour and Museum is the place for you. You can see the changing rooms and the players' lounge and learn about the history of the club.

When Jack comes to stay, we often go to the Museum of Science and Industry. My favourite is the Air and Space Hall. There are models of spacecraft, with spacesuits, food and equipment. Jack liked the special exhibition about the Blackfoot Indians.

I also like the Lowry Centre. L. S. Lowry was born in Manchester in 1887. He painted the streets and factories around his home.

Module 4

It's different!

In Module 4 you study

Grammar

- Comparatives:
  -er than / more ... than,
  It isn't as ... as ... , Is it as ... as ... ?
- Possessive pronouns
- Superlatives
- The future with *going to*
- The comparative and superlative of *good* and *bad*

Vocabulary

- Adjectives
- Names of modern inventions
- Questions with *How* + adjective ... ?

so that you can

- Describe and compare things
- Talk about similarities and differences
- Compare different ways of life
- Talk about people's possessions
- Compare one thing with the rest of a group
- Make questions about places you know
- Talk about future plans and intentions
- Describe plans for a trip
- Compare things and give your opinion

Swim!

Chapter 1 – You don't understand!
Chapter 2 – Emily's ambition

Life and culture

Poem – Mum, Dad and Me
The longest road in the world

Coursework 4

Superlative places!
You draw a map of your country and write about places there.

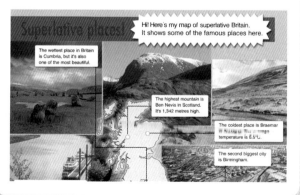

What's it about?

What can you say about the pictures?

Now match the pictures with sentences 1–5.

1 It's more interesting than our house.
2 Whose is this camera?
3 The most dangerous animal in the world.
4 Kate's going to work in the USA.
5 How big is the Sahara?

In Step 1 you study
- adjectives
- comparative adjectives

so that you can
- describe and compare things

1 Key vocabulary *Adjectives*

a 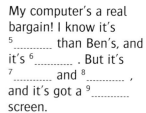 Listen and say the words.

big   cheap   expensive   fast   short
new   old   powerful   long   slow
small   tall   young

⏱ You've got four minutes! Look at the adjectives in the list and find:

1 short — long or tall

1 Two words with two opposites.
2 Three pairs of opposites.
3 One word without an opposite.

b Choose at least three adjectives from the list and make sentences to show their meaning.

Cheetahs have got very powerful legs.

2 Presentation *It's faster and more powerful*

a Read the two adverts. What are Ben and Lisa selling? Is Ben's computer the same as Lisa's?

b Now read the sentences. Which is Lisa's computer? Which is Ben's?

1 Ben's computer.

1 It's slower.
2 It's faster and more powerful.
3 The screen is smaller.
4 It's newer.
5 It's more expensive.
6 It's older.
7 The screen is bigger.
8 It's cheaper.

c Complete what Ben and Lisa say.

Buy my computer!
I know it's ¹ *slower*
than Lisa's, and it's got a
² _____ screen. But it's
³ _____ and it's ⁴ _____ .
It's a real bargain!

My computer's a real
bargain! I know it's
⁵ _____ than Ben's, and
it's ⁶ _____ . But it's
⁷ _____ and ⁸ _____ ,
and it's got a ⁹ _____
screen.

 Listen and check.

NOTICE BOARD

FOR SALE
Nekta computer

1.5 GHz

17" screen

3 years old

£249

A real bargain!

Contact Lisa Carter Class 9DW

email lisalcarter@interlink.co.uk

FOR SALE

A real bargain!

Tango computer

1.2 GHz

15" screen

2 years old

£199

Ben Wilson Class 9PG
Telephone 01352 412197
email benthebeast@communiK8.com

3 Key grammar *Comparatives*

Complete the examples and read the explanation.

Lisa's computer is
| faster
| old...........
| more expensive .... Ben's.
| .... powerful

To form comparative adjectives, we add -er (or -r), or we put more *before the adjective.*

See Spelling notes, page 143.

G→ 22a-c

4 Practice

a Write the comparative form of these adjectives.

1 more beautiful   2 bigger

1 beautiful   2 big   3 dangerous   4 long
5 difficult   6 important   7 short   8 small
9 intelligent   10 young   11 interesting   12 tall

b Make complete sentences.

1 Japanese is more difficult than English.

1 Japanese / difficult / English
2 Beth / tall / Kim
3 Tom's hair / long / Dean's
4 love / important / money
5 Lucy / old / Robbie
6 Kim's skirt / short / Beth's

c **Test a friend** Write another example for 4b. Can your friend make a complete sentence?

you / tall / me

> You're taller than me.

5 Key pronunciation /ə/

🔲 Listen to the rhythm drill, then join in. Practise the /ə/ sound.

A: Is it bigger?   B: Yes, it's bigger.
A: Is it longer?   B: Yes, it's longer.
A: Is it faster?   B: Yes, it's faster.
A: Is it newer?   B: Yes, it's newer.
A: Is it better?   B: Yes, it's better.
A: And is it cheaper?   B: No, it's more expensive.

....
Try this!
Can you find the adjectives?
SMLL LNG DFFCLT BLCK GRY GRN FST
YNG BTFL FSCNTNG CHP XPNSV
....

6 Key vocabulary *Computers*

Match the words with the numbers.

screen   printer   speaker   keyboard   mouse

🔲 Listen and check.

7 Listening and speaking *Sold?*

a 🔲 Listen to the telephone conversation. What does Helen want to do?

b 🔲 Read the questions, then listen again and find the answers.

1 Is Ben selling the keyboard and the mouse?
2 Are there any speakers?
3 Is the printer for sale?
4 How much does Helen want to pay?
5 When is she going to see the computer?

c **Role play** If you have time, act the conversation between Ben and Helen.

8 Writing and speaking *A real bargain*

Use what you know

Work with a friend. Choose something to sell: *a computer, a CD player, a car.* Then work separately. Write your own advert with the price, the age and at least one other detail. Compare your two adverts, then try to sell your 'bargain' to the class.

> My car's cheaper than Ella's, and it's a nicer colour. It's a real bargain!

In Step 2 you study
- names of modern inventions
- *It isn't as ... as ... / Is it as ... as ... ?*

so that you can
- talk about similarities and differences
- compare different ways of life

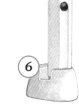

1 Key vocabulary *Modern inventions*

Match the words with the pictures. You've got one minute!

digital camera   DVD player   fridge
electric toothbrush   microwave   stereo
washing machine   hairdryer

Listen and check.

2 Reading *It's paradise!*

a Read about Richie Sowa. Why isn't Richie's island an ordinary island?

The Adventures of Robinson Crusoe is the story of life on a desert island nearly three hundred years ago. Richie Sowa, from Middlesbrough in the UK, is a 21st century Robinson Crusoe. His home is an island near Cancun in Mexico. But Richie's island is different. He built it himself – with 250,000 plastic bottles!

The house has got a living room, a simple kitchen and two bedrooms. The weather is hot, dry and sunny so Richie uses solar power. He's got a solar cooker, a shower, electric lights and a CD player. He shares the island with his dog, two ducks and four cats.

A lot of tourists visit the island and, last year, an ecology student stayed there and studied Richie's way of life. 'It's paradise!' he said.

b Read the article again and find the answers to these questions.

1 What did Richie use to build his house?
2 How many rooms has he got?
3 Is the weather good?
4 How does Richie cook his food?
5 Has he got a lot of modern machines?

3 Presentation *It isn't as nice as our house*

a 🔊 Close your books and listen to George and Marlene. Do they agree about Richie's island?

George and Marlene are American tourists from Detroit. They're visiting Richie Sowa's home.

MARLENE: Wow! Our house isn't as interesting as this, George! Why don't we build an island?

GEORGE: You must be joking! Our house is more comfortable than this crazy place.

MARLENE: The weather's nicer here, George.

GEORGE: OK, so the weather isn't as nice in Detroit, but at least we've got a fridge and a washing machine.

MARLENE: I don't mind about that, George. It's quieter here, and the air's cleaner. It's paradise!

GEORGE: Well, I like Detroit. Maybe it isn't as beautiful as this place, but we've got three TVs and there's a supermarket next door.

MARLENE: But, George, is our life as exciting as Richie's?

GEORGE: You're crazy, Marlene. I'm hot. Let's go back to the coach.

b 🔊 Listen again and follow in your book. Then read these sentences. Are they about Richie's home or George and Marlene's?

1 George and Marlene's home.

1 It isn't as interesting.
2 It's more comfortable.
3 The weather isn't as nice.
4 It's warmer and sunnier.
5 It isn't as modern.
6 It's noisier and more polluted.
7 It isn't as beautiful.

4 Key grammar *as ... as ...*

a Complete the examples, then complete the explanation.

b How do you say the sentences in your language?

Is our life		exciting		Richie's?
Our house isn't	-------	nice	-------	Richie's.

When we compare two things, we use as + *adjective* + ...

G ➤ 23

5 Practice

a Make two sentences for each number.

1 Detroit isn't as hot as Cancun. Cancun's hotter than Detroit.

1 Detroit / hot / Cancun
2 Richie's house / comfortable / George and Marlene's
3 Detroit / sunny / Cancun
4 Marlene's house / interesting / Richie's island
5 Cancun / noisy / Detroit
6 villages / polluted / big cities

b **Test a friend** Write another example for 5a. Can your friend make a sentence with *as ... as ...* ?

Indian elephants / big / African elephants

> Indian elephants aren't as big as African elephants.

6 Speaking and writing *Comparisons*

Use what you know

Work with a friend and compare these things. How many sentences can you make with *isn't/aren't as ... as ...* ?

Cats aren't as friendly as dogs.

cats / dogs

my home/ the Taj Mahal

geography / chemistry

England / my country

In Step 3 you study
- possessive pronouns
- *Whose ... ?*

so that you can
- talk about people's possessions

1 Presentation *Yours or mine?*

a 🔊 Listen to the conversation and follow in your book. What's the problem?

Marlene, George and their friends are at the cathedral in Mexico City. It's the end of their visit and they're getting their cameras.

GEORGE: I can't find my camera.

JOHN: Well, I've got mine. Is this yours, George?

GEORGE: No, that's Marlene's. Mine is bigger than hers.

MARLENE: Thanks, John.

JOHN: Pete and Nancy, have you got yours?

NANCY: Yes, thanks, John. It's on the coach.

JOHN: Well, whose is this camera?

GEORGE: Ask Marcie and Bill. I think it's theirs.

MARCIE: Yes, it's ours. Thanks, John.

JOHN: OK. So have we all got our cameras?

MARLENE: No, we haven't. George can't find his.

b Are these sentences true or false? Correct the false sentences.

1 George has got his camera.
2 John hasn't got his camera.
3 Marlene has got hers.
4 Pete and Nancy's camera is on the coach.
5 John is holding Marcie and Bill's camera.

2 Key grammar *Possessive pronouns*

Complete the table.

Possessive adjectives	Possessive pronouns
my	mine
your	1 _____
2 _____	his
her	3 _____
our	4 _____
5 _____	yours
their	6 _____

Whose is this camera?

It's Marlene's camera. *or* It's Marlene's.

 **G** ➔ 26a-b, 27a-c

3 Practice

a Change the underlined words. Write sentences with a possessive pronoun.

1 I think this is his.

1 Ben's bag is green. I think this is <u>his bag</u>.
2 Lisa's got a camera. Perhaps you can use <u>her camera</u>.
3 Whose are these trainers? Are they <u>your trainers</u>?
4 Joe and Sadie have got a new printer. <u>Their printer</u> is faster than <u>our printer</u>.
5 Are these your sunglasses? – No, they aren't <u>my sunglasses</u>.

b Complete the sentences with a possessive pronoun.

1 Where's Lisa? This notebook is _.hers_. .
2 Whose is this skateboard? Ben, is it _____ ?
3 Is this your toothbrush? – No. It isn't _____ .
4 We've got our tickets. Mike and Sue, have you got _____ ?
5 I haven't got a map. Have Joe and Sadie got _____ ?
6 Is this Jack's tennis racket? – No. _____ is in the car.
7 We've got numbers 45 and 46. Those seats are _____ .

c Write questions and answers. Use *this, these* and the possessive *'s*.

1 Whose is this camera? – It's Marlene's.

1 camera / Marlene
2 jacket / Matt
3 rucksack / Lisa
4 trainers / Ben

4 Writing and speaking *A conversation*

Use what you know

Work in a group. Write a conversation like the one in 1a, then act it. Change the names and change *camera* to *bag*.

Swim!

CHAPTER 1

You don't understand

'Well done, Emily,' said Jack Hastings. 'Faster than yesterday!'

'Thanks, Jack!' Emily replied. She took a drink of water from her water bottle. Emily and Jack were in the small café at the Lakeside swimming pool. The pool was the home of the Lakeside Dolphins Swimming Club. Jack was the club trainer and Emily swam there every day.

'Er,' said Jack, suddenly serious, 'I want to talk to you about something…'

Emily looked at her watch and stood up quickly. 'Sorry, Jack, I can't. It's eight o'clock,' she said. 'Tomorrow?'

Emily ran to the bus stop and got the bus home to the village of Picton. She knew that her father was waiting for her. As she opened the front door of her house, she began to feel unhappy. As she went into the house, she felt very unhappy.

'You're late!' Anthony James came to the door and looked at his daughter.

'Sorry,' said Emily.

'And what about your homework?'

Emily didn't say anything.

'You know Emily,' said her father, 'you only think about swimming, swimming and more swimming. What about school?'

Her father was always like this. He just didn't understand. 'But Dad …'

'What about going to university? What about becoming a lawyer?'

'I told you, I don't want to be a lawyer,' said Emily.

'You're being very stupid, Emily!' said her father. 'And your mother …'

Emily ran upstairs to her bedroom. She lay on her bed. She thought about her mother and cried.

She cried for a long time.

Questions

1 Who is the main character in the story? What can you say about her?
2 Who are Jack Hastings and Anthony James?
3 Do you think Emily and her father often argue?

Extra exercises

1 Choose the right words.

1 These shirts aren't clean. Put them in the _____ .
   a fridge
   b washing machine
   c toothbrush

2 I want to buy a _____ camera.
   a digital
   b DVD
   c solar

3 A _____ cooks food very fast.
   a printer
   b player
   c microwave

4 We need a new _____ for our computer.
   a screen
   b stereo
   c speakers

5 Don't swim here! The water is _____ .
   a clean
   b polluted
   c powerful

6 This CD player was _____ . It was a real bargain!
   a important
   b expensive
   c cheap

2 Put the letters in the right order and make the opposites of adjectives 1–8.

wols   gunoy   teqiu   telteniling   horts   cluftifid   lamsl   bongri

1 noisy *quiet*   5 interesting
2 fast   6 stupid
3 big   7 easy
4 old   8 long

3 Complete the sentences. Use the comparative form of the adjectives + *than*.

1 Danny's eyes are *darker than* mine. (*dark*)
2 Your bedroom is _____ Jenny's. (*big*)
3 A computer screen is _____ a mouse. (*expensive*)
4 The book was _____ the film. (*exciting*)
5 Spain is _____ England. (*sunny*)
6 I think mobile phones are _____ calculators. (*useful*)

4 Make sentences. Use *isn't/aren't* + *as ... as*.

1 *Alex isn't as old as David.*
1 Alex is younger than David.
2 You're shorter than Rosie.
3 Keyboards are cheaper than printers.
4 A bicycle is slower than a car.
5 Cheetahs are smaller than lions.
6 The science exam is easier than the maths exam.

5 Complete the conversations. Choose a or b.

A: Look at Anne's photos. They're great!
B: [1] _____ are good too, I think.
A: But [2] _____ are fantastic. They're a lot more interesting than [3] _____ .

A: Is that [4] _____ car outside?
B: No, that car belongs to my uncle. [5] _____ is the green Peugeot.

A: [6] _____ is this tent?
B: I'm not sure. Ask Jack and Ben. It think it's [7] _____ .

1 a You   b Yours
2 a she   b hers
3 a my   b mine
4 a your   b yours
5 a Our   b Ours
6 a Whose   b Who's
7 a theirs   b there's

6 How do you say these sentences in your language?

1 It's a real bargain!
2 It isn't for sale.
3 You must be joking!
4 At least we've got a fridge.
5 I don't mind about that.
6 How much is it?

Extra reading

Poem

Do you ever read poetry? Do you know the names of any famous poets in your country?

Task

Answer the questions and talk about the poem with your friends.

1 How old is the writer of the poem? Guess.
2 Where do he and his parents live now?
3 Where did his parents live before?
4 Which way of life is better – what does the writer think? What do you think?

Mum, Dad and Me

My parents grew among palm trees,
in sunshine strong and clear.
I grow in weather that's pale,
misty, watery or plain cold,
around the back streets in London.

Dad swam in warm sea, at my age.
I swim in a roofed pool.
Mum – she still doesn't swim.

Mum went to an open village market
at my age. I go to a covered
arcade one with her now.
Dad works most Saturdays.

At my age Dad played
cricket with friends.
Mum helped her mum, or talked
shouting half way up a hill.
Now I read or talk on the phone.

With her friends, Mum's mum washed
clothes on a river-stone. Now
washing-machine washes our clothes.
We save time to eat to TV[1],
never speaking.

My dad longed for freedom in Jamaica.
I want a greater freedom.
Mum prays for us, always.

Mum goes to church
some evenings and on Sundays.
I go to the library.
Dad goes for his darts at the local[2].

Mum walked everywhere, at my age.
Dad rode a donkey.
Now I take the bus
or catch the underground train.

from *When I Dance* by James Berry

[1] to eat in front of the TV
[2] the local pub

ABOUT IMMIGRATION

In the 1950s, hundreds of people from the Caribbean came to Britain, hoping for a better life.

8 Our incredible world

STEP 1

In Step 1 you study
- questions with *How* + adjective ... ?
- superlatives

so that you can
- compare one thing with the rest of a group
- make questions about places you know

The River Nile

Our solar system

1 Key vocabulary *How long is it?*

a 🕐 Look at the photos, then match the questions with the right answers. You've got three minutes! *1c*

1 How long is the River Nile?
2 How old is the Earth?
3 How tall is the CN Tower?
4 How high is Mount Everest?
5 How big is the Sahara Desert?
6 How far can a flea jump?
7 How dangerous is the poison arrow frog?
8 How large is a 747 jet?

a It's about 4,600 million years old.
b It's 2,000 kilometres from north to south and 5,000 kilometres from east to west.
c It's 6,695 kilometres long.
d It's 8,848 metres high.
e 33 centimetres. That's 220 times the size of its body!
f It's 553 metres tall.
g It can carry more than 500 people.
h It's very dangerous. The poison from one frog can kill a hundred people.

A 747 jumbo jet

The CN Tower in Toronto, Canada

b Work with a friend. Ask and answer the questions.

> How long is the River Nile?

> It's 6,695 kilometres long.

 Listen and check.

Remember!

We use *How tall ... ?* for people, trees and buildings.
We use *How high ... ?* for buildings and mountains.

Big and *large* have got the same meaning.

2 Presentation
The biggest and the most amazing!

Look at the photos again, then match the descriptions with the right names.

1 *The Nile is the longest river in the world.*

1 It's longer than the Amazon and the Mississippi. It's the longest river in the world.
2 It's the tallest building in the world.
3 It's the largest plane in the world.
4 It's the highest mountain in the world.
5 It's the biggest desert in the world.
6 It's the most amazing athlete in the animal kingdom.
7 It's the most dangerous animal in the world.

 Listen and check.

Mount Everest

The poison arrow frog

A flea

The Sahara Desert

4 Practice

a Write the superlative form of these adjectives.

1 coldest   2 most expensive

1 cold 2 expensive 3 small 4 intelligent
5 popular 6 old 7 short

b Make true sentences with the adjectives in 4a.

1 The *most expensive* car in the world is the Mercedes CLK/LM. It costs $1.5m.
2 The .... day of the year is December 21st.
3 The .... university in the world is in Morocco. It opened more than 1000 years ago.
4 The gorilla is one of the .... animals in the world. It can use sign language.
5 The .... boy's name in the USA is Michael.
6 Antarctica is the .... place in the world.
7 The .... planet in our solar system is Pluto.

c **Test a friend** Write another sentence for 4b. Can your friend complete the sentence?

The .... country in the world is the Vatican City.

> The smallest country in the world is the Vatican City.

3 Key grammar *Superlatives*

Complete the examples, and read the explanation.

	largest		
It's the	long...........	plane	in the world.
	most amazing	river	
	.... dangerous	place	

To form the superlative, we add -est (or -st), or we put most *before the adjective.*

See Spelling notes, page 143.

G 22a-c

Try this!
What is it?
When it is born, it is as big as a house.
It drinks 100 litres of milk a day.
Its heart is the same size as a small car.
Its mother is the same length as a 737 jet.

5 Key pronunciation /ɪ/ *and* /iː/

[🔊] Listen and repeat the words.

1 /ɪ/ sit chip live it
2 /iː/ seat cheap leave eat

[🔊] Now listen and say these words. Are they the same or different?

1 biggest beach *different* 2 flea tree
3 city street 4 rich sing
5 meat milk 6 drink dream

6 Writing and speaking *Places you know*

Use what you know

Ask your friends at least two questions about places in your country or your town.

What's the longest river in ... ?
What's the most popular café in ... ?

STEP 2

In Step 2 you study
- the future with *going to*

so that you can
- talk about future plans and intentions
- describe plans for a trip

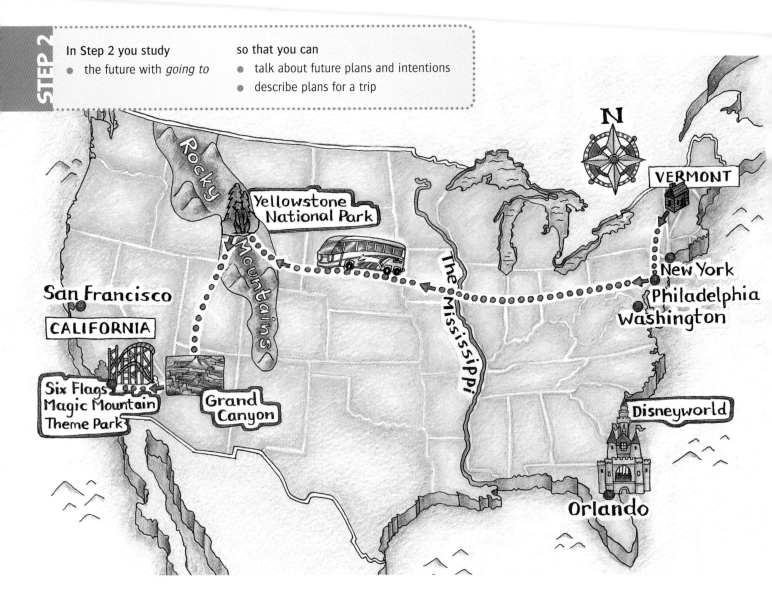

1 Presentation *What are they going to do?*

a Look at the map of the USA. How many of the names do you know?

b Read about Kate's plans, then look at the map and put sentences a–e in the right order.

My name's Kate Kelly and I'm a student at Bristol University. Next summer I'm going to spend two months in the States. I'm going to work at Camp America in Vermont. I'm going to teach swimming and diving.

a   I want to go to the Yellowstone National Park and see the bears there.

b   After that I'm going to stay with my relatives in Philadelphia.

c   At the end of our holiday, we're going to spend a couple of days at the Six Flags Magic Mountain in California. It's a theme park, and it's got the fastest roller coaster in the States!

d   After that we're going to visit the Grand Canyon.

e   Then my cousin Monica and I are going to travel across America on a Greyhound Bus.

🔊 Listen and check.

c Are these sentences true or false? Correct the false sentences.

1   Kate's in the States at the moment.

2   She's going to work as a sports teacher there.

3   She isn't going to spend two months at Camp America.

4   Kate and Monica are going to fly across the States.

5   They're going to see the bears in the Yellowstone National Park.

6   They aren't going to visit any theme parks.

2 Key grammar *going to*

Look at the examples, then complete the explanation.

I'm Kate isn't	going to	travel by bus. visit New York.
Are you When are they		be a teacher? leave?

We use be + ... + *verb when we talk about future plans and intentions.*

G ➔ 8

3 Practice

Make sentences with the right form of *going to*.

1 *Kate isn't going to stay in America.*
   She's going to go back to Bristol.

1 Kate / stay in America. She / go back to Bristol.
2 What / Kate / teach ?
3 she / see her relatives ?
4 you / travel by coach ?
5 I / take any photos. I haven't got my camera.
6 Monica and Kate / go by train. They / get a Greyhound bus.
7 they / visit the Niagara Falls ?
8 Where / they / spend the weekend ?
9 What / they / do ?
10 they / visit any theme parks ?

4 Speaking

What about you? Work with a friend and ask and answer questions like these.

What are you going to do after school?
What are you going to do next weekend?
Are you going to watch the football tonight?

> What are you going to do tonight?

> I'm going to play basketball.

5 Listening and speaking *It's a bear!*

George and Marlene are camping in the Yellowstone National Park.

a Look at the picture and copy these words. Which words are in the conversation? Guess.

tent   camera   attack   bear   sandwiches   photo   rucksack   watch   eat

b 🔲 Listen to George and Marlene. Tick the words in your list when you hear them.   bear ✓

c 🔲 Listen again, then complete the conversation.

MARLENE: George, look! There's a ¹............ over there!
GEORGE: A ²............ ! Oh my goodness! It's going to ³............ us, Marlene!
MARLENE: Don't panic, George. It's fine.
GEORGE: Fine? What ⁴............ do?
MARLENE: Well, I'm ⁵............ stay here and ⁶............ it.
GEORGE: Look! It's going to ⁷............ .
MARLENE: Never mind, dear. I'm ⁸............ my ⁹............ . I'm ¹⁰............ .
GEORGE: You're crazy, Marlene!

d **Role play** If you have time, act the conversation between Marlene and George.

6 Writing and speaking *Plans for a trip*

Use what you know

Imagine you're going to go on an exciting trip. Write answers to these questions.

How are you going to get there?
What are you going to take?
Where are you going to stay?
What are you going to visit?
What else are you going to do?

Read your answers to a friend. Can your friend guess where you're going?

In Step 3 you study
- the comparative and superlative of *good* and *bad*

so that you can
- compare things and give your opinion

1 Presentation *Which telescope is the best?*

Look at the information. Then read the sentences. Which telescope is it?

I'm going to buy a new telescope.

TELESCOPES THIS WEEK'S BEST BUYS

Zoomi ✪✪✪✪ £229
Kent ✪✪✪ £245
Telstar ✪✪ £178
Delta ✪ £119

1 It's got four stars. That's the best rating.
2 It's the cheapest, but it's got the worst rating.
3 It's more expensive than the Zoomi but it isn't as good.
4 It isn't as good as the Kent but it's better than the Delta.

🔲 Listen and check.

2 Key grammar *good/better/best*

Complete the table.

	Comparative	Superlative
good	....	the best
bad	worse	....

The comparative and superlative of good *and* bad *are irregular.*

G → 22d

3 Practice

Look at the hotel ratings, then complete the sentences with words from the grammar box.

The Silver Beach ★★★★ **The Grand Hotel** ★★★

The Sahara ★★ **The Coach House** ★

1 The Silver Beach has got the .... rating.
2 The Coach House has got the .... rating.
3 The Grand Hotel isn't as .... as the Silver Beach but it's .... than the Sahara.
4 The Sahara's rating is .... than the Grand's.

4 Reading *Amazing!*

a Read Matt's essay and choose a title.

a The sky at night.
b My favourite pastime.
c A holiday in Cornwall.

English

Matt Long Class 9

My main interest is astronomy – the study of the stars. When I was little, I always watched a programme called 'The sky at night'. There was a lot of information about the eclipse of the sun in August 1999. The best place to see it was Cornwall. So we all went to Cornwall on holiday, but the weather was awful. We didn't see the eclipse because it was too cloudy. I was very disappointed, and everyone said it was our worst holiday.

   I bought a new telescope last week. Last night I got up at four o'clock because I wanted to see the International Space Station. It was travelling at 28,000 kilometres an hour, 386 kilometres above my head. I could see it clearly. Amazing!

b Answer these questions.

1 Why did Matt and his family go to Cornwall?
2 What was the problem?
3 Did they have a good holiday?
4 Has Matt got a new telescope?
5 What was one of his best moments?

5 Speaking and writing *Your opinion*

Use what you know

Read the questions, then share your opinions.

Who's the best singer in your country? What's the most interesting place / the nicest food / the best drink? Where's the best weather? **Imagine you're telling a visitor about your country. Write your recommendations.**

The best drink in our country is 'maté'.

Swim!

CHAPTER 2

Emily's ambition

The next evening, Emily swam faster than ever before. The cool water on her body felt good. Afterwards, Jack said: 'Emily, do you want to be a professional swimmer one day?'

'Do I want to be a professional swimmer?' said Emily. 'You know that I do.'

'What a question!' she thought. It was her dream, a dream that started when she was six years old.

'Well,' said Jack, 'today is July 1st and on August 15th there's a race across the lake …'

'The Picton Lake Race? But isn't it just for women … not girls?' asked Emily.

'Well, competitors must be at least fourteen, and you're fourteen now!' Jack answered.

It was true. Emily's birthday was on June 20th.

'Isn't that the race that Tina Dawson always wins?' she asked Jack. Tina Dawson was a former European Champion. She lived near Picton and she was still a very good swimmer.

Jack smiled. 'Four times,' he said. 'But not this year!'

Emily smiled at Jack. Then suddenly she felt sad.

'What's the matter?' asked Jack.

'It's Dad,' she said, and she told Jack the story. 'Mum died five years ago, and he wants me to be just like her, but I don't want to be a lawyer.'

Jack looked at Emily kindly.

'He doesn't understand that swimming is the most important thing in the world for me,' she said. 'But if I win the Picton Lake Race …!' Then Emily started to think. 'But what about training? If I train more …'

'Well,' said Jack, 'we could train early in the morning, before you go to school.'

When Jack said 'we', Emily started to feel happier. 'Really?' she asked.

Jack laughed. 'We can start tomorrow!'

Questions

1 What's Emily's ambition?
2 Why is August 15th an important date?
3 Who won the race last year?

Extra exercises

1 Complete the questions. Use *How* + the adjectives in the list + *is/are*.

tall   heavy   long   big   far   high

1 A: *How big is* your computer?
   B: It's quite small. I can carry it in my bag.
2 A: .... that mountain?
   B: About 1,200 metres.
3 A: .... the Elbe River?
   B: 1,145 kilometres.
4 A: .... those trees?
   B: About 15 metres, I think.
5 A: .... we from home?
   B: Don't worry! We're nearly there now.
6 A: .... your rucksack?
   B: I don't know, but I don't think I can carry it!

2 Choose the right words.

1 Their garden is about 18 metres ....
   a high
   b long
   c big
2 I'm the .... member of my family.
   a tallest
   b taller
   c highest
3 I think this is .... beautiful beach on the south coast.
   a more
   b most
   c the most
4 Your art project is .... than mine.
   a best
   b better
   c the worst
5 A: The weather's awful!
   B: Yes, but it isn't as .... as yesterday.
   a bad
   b worse
   c worst
6 I think Mrs Thomas is the .... teacher in the school. She's really nice.
   a good
   b better
   c best

3 Complete the sentences. Use the superlative form of the adjectives.

1 Lake Superior is the .... lake in America. (*big*)
2 Ali is one of the .... students in my class. Everyone likes him. (*popular*)
3 My .... subject is geography. I only got 32% in the last exam! (*bad*)
4 This is the .... flat in the building because it's near the road. (*noisy*)
5 Libya is the .... country in the world. In the summer it's sometimes 58°C. (*hot*)
6 You can't buy that jacket. It's the .... thing in the shop! (*expensive*)
7 We always go out and have a good time on Saturday. It's the .... day of the week. (*good*)

4 Put the words in the right order and make sentences.

1 *I'm going to travel with Veronica.*
1 travel / Veronica / going / I'm / with / to
2 tent / going / Mike's / in / sleep / to / a
3 any / buy / aren't / to / We / going / clothes
4 library / to / us / outside / going / meet / the / They're
5 in / stay / not / a / I'm / to / hotel / going
6 invite / her / to / you / going / Jane's / party / to

5 Complete the conversations. Use *going to*.

A: [1]........................ the day in London? (*you / spend*)
B: Yes, [2]........................ my cousin Sarah. (*I / see*)
   [3]........................ me at Victoria Station. (*She / meet*)
A: What [4]........................? (*you / do*)
B: [5]........................ a boat trip down the river. (*We / take*)

A: [6]........................ to France? (*your parents / drive*)
B: No, [7]........................ the car. (*they / not take*)
   [8]........................ for some cheap plane tickets on the Internet. (*Dad / look*)

6 How do you say these sentences in your language?

1 Oh, my goodness!
2 Don't panic.
3 Never mind.
4 How are you going to get there?
5 What else are you going to do?
6 How long is its body?

Extra reading

The longest road in the world

Close your book and imagine you're travelling down the west coast of North and South America. How many places can you think of?

My name's Hank Weaver. I'm a truck driver. I sometimes travel on the Pan-American Highway. It's the longest road in the world. Why don't you come with me?

The highway goes from Alaska in the north to Chile in the south. It goes through 12 different countries and it's 16,000 miles long. It goes past lakes and volcanoes, through snow and desert, hills and valleys, jungles and mountains.

California's Pacific coast is my favourite part of the route. Do you know the name of this famous bridge? It's in San Francisco – one of the biggest cities on the highway.

When I'm in Arizona, I always stop for a meal at the Highway Diner. They make the best apple pie in the world.

Have a look at this! Isn't it beautiful? It's a Blue Morpho butterfly and it lives in the rainforests of Central and South America.

Between Panama and Colombia, there is no highway for 54 miles. This is called the Darien Gap. Some people want to build a road here. But a lot of people don't want the road because this is one of the richest and most important regions for wildlife in the world.

I'm going to take the ferry now, to the next section of the highway. I mean, you can't go and drive through someone's garden, can you!

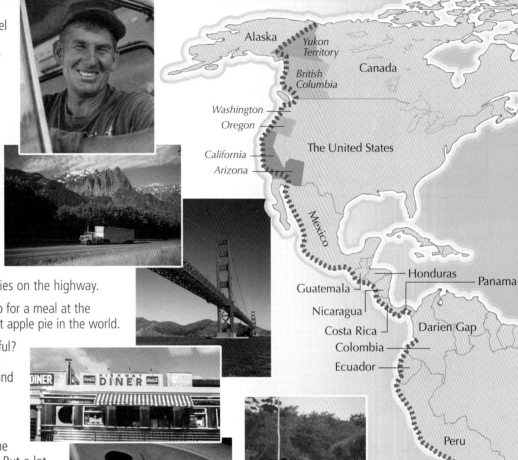

ıııııı Pan American Highway

ABOUT AMERICAN ENGLISH

Sometimes American English and British English are different.

American	British
highway	road
truck	lorry
apartment	flat
movie	film

Task

Read the text and find the following things.

1 A cold place.
2 A city on the coast of California.
3 A hot, dry place.
4 Something to eat.
5 A rare and beautiful insect.
6 A country in Central America.
7 An important area for wildlife.

Module 4 Review

Language summary

Park View	New York Hilton	Crystal Palace
$250 a night	$900 a night	$25,000 a night

The New York Hilton is more expensive than the Park View but it isn't as expensive as the Crystal Palace.
The Crystal Palace is the most expensive hotel in the world.

1 Comparative and superlative adjectives

Pete	Claire	John

Claire is taller than Pete but she isn't as tall as John.
John is the tallest boy in his class.

2nd	1st	3rd
Rosie	Claire	Helen

Rosie is better than Helen but she isn't as good as Claire.
Claire is the best athlete in the competition.

451/2000	239/2000	104/2000
John	Holly	Pete

Holly's score is worse than John's but it isn't as bad as Pete's.
Pete's score is the worst of all.

Spelling		
nice	nicer	the nicest
large	larger	the largest
big	bigger	the biggest
lazy	lazier	the laziest
friendly	friendlier	the friendliest

Check that you can

1.1 ● make comparisons.
Write complete sentences with these adjectives.

hot   long   polluted   big
dangerous   good

1 *The Earth is bigger than Venus but it isn't as big as Jupiter.*
1 The Earth / Venus / Jupiter
2 The Mississippi / the Thames / the Nile
3 The Earth / Mars / Mercury
4 Athens / London / Hong Kong
5 Matt's essay / Claire's / Mirela's
6 surfing / running / skydiving

1.2 ● use superlative adjectives.
Make questions, then ask and answer.

1 *What's the longest wall in the world?*
1 What's / long wall / in the world ?
2 What's / intelligent animal / in the world ?
3 Where's / tall building / in your town ?
4 Where are / good shops / in your town ?
5 Who's / old person / in the class ?
6 Who's / important person / in your life ?
7 What's / bad day / of the week ?
8 What's / good day / of the week ?

2 How + adjective

How	big high difficult	is it?

Check that you can

● ask for a description with *How*.
For each sentence, make a question with: *How* + adjective + *is ...* ?

1 *How difficult is the Tour de France?*
1 The Tour de France is very difficult.
2 The Mississippi is 6,210 kilometres long.
3 The Grand Hotel has got 364 rooms and two restaurants.
4 Joe is 1.75 metres tall.
5 The Greyhound Bus travels at about 80 kilometres an hour.
6 Mount McKinley is 6,194 metres high.

3 Possessive pronouns and *Whose ... ?*

Possessive pronouns can come before or after the verb:

*I like your watch. **Yours** is nicer than mine.*
***Ours** is over there. I can't see **theirs**.*

Possessive adjectives	Possessive pronouns
my camera	It's **mine**.
your sisters	They're **yours**.
his anorak	That's **his**.
her idea	It's **hers**.
its legs	–
our bag	It's **ours**.
your stereo	It's **yours**.
their car	This is **theirs**.

I like Ben's bike, but I prefer **Jack's**. It isn't Pete and Jane's dog. It's **Joe and Sadie's**.

We use *Whose ... ?* to ask about possessions.

Whose	is this camera?
	are those trainers?

Check that you can

● use possessive pronouns.

Complete the conversations with the pronouns in the box.

1 A: Whose is this pencil case?
   B: Ask Matt. I think it's ....
2 A: Whose are these glasses?
   B: Ask Sadie. I think they're
   ....
3 A: Are these your boots?
   B: No, they aren't. .... are here.
4 A: Jack and Ben, is this your football?
   B: No, it isn't ....
5 A: Whose is this rucksack?
   B: Ask Dave and Nancy. I think it's ....
6 A: I think you've got my calculator.
   B: No, this isn't ....

4 The future with *going to*

We use *going to* + verb to talk about intentions and plans.

Affirmative

I'm/He's/She's/ We're/You're/They're	going to	take some photos. buy a new computer. be in Tom's team.

Negative

I'm not/He isn't/ She isn't/We aren't/ You aren't/They aren't	going to	buy a new car. vote for Bilaggio. visit the cathedral.

Questions and answers

Is he/she	going to invite Pete?
Are we/you/they	

Yes, I am.	No, I'm not.
Yes, he/she is.	No, he/she isn't.
Yes, we/you/they are.	No, we/you/they aren't.

Check that you can

● describe future plans and intentions.

Match the questions in A with the answers in B, then work with a friend and make six conversations.

A
1 Are you thirsty?
2 What does Jack want to do?
3 Which hairdryer are you going to buy?
4 The Belair campsite is awful.
5 Why are they wearing shorts?
6 Do you like Hannah Brown?

B
a I know. We aren't going to stay there.
b The Bran 66. It's got the best rating.
c Yes, I'm going to have some juice.
d They're going to play tennis.
e I'm not going to tell you.
f He's going to go on the roller coaster.

5 *Who is / Who has / Whose*

Who's Harry Potter? = Who is Harry Potter?
Who's got my ruler? = Who has got my ruler?
Whose is this pen? = Who does this pen belong to?

Be careful! They've all got the same sound!

Check that you can

● use these three different forms.

Complete the sentences with *Who is, Who has* or *Whose.*

1 .... is this anorak? – It's Pete's.
2 .... Frodo Baggins? – He's in *The Lord of the Rings*.
3 .... got the new Beyoncé CD? – Mel's got it.
4 .... in your group? – John, Ben, Helen and Jane.
5 .... are these socks? – They're mine.
6 And .... are those? – I think they're Joe's.

Vocabulary

Adjectives
big
cheap
dangerous
difficult
easy
expensive
fast
far (*adj./adv.*)
high
important
intelligent
interesting
long
new
old
powerful
short
slow
small
tall
young

Computers
keyboard
mouse
printer
screen
speaker

Modern inventions
CD player
cooker
digital camera
DVD player
electric toothbrush
fridge
hairdryer
light
microwave
shower
stereo
washing machine

Going on a trip
bus
camera
coach
(to) fly
national park
photo
roller coaster
rucksack
(to) spend (time)
(to) stay (with someone)
theme park
train
(to) travel
(to) visit

Expressions
You must be joking.
It's a real bargain.
At least ... .
How are you going
  to get there?
I don't mind.
Oh my goodness!
Never mind.

Study skills 4
Recognising sentence patterns

Different sorts of sentences usually follow the same 'pattern'.
🕐 Complete these sentences with the words in the lists.
You've got five minutes!

Affirmative sentences   is   has   wants   visited

1 Lisa .... a DVD player.
2 Matt .... writing a letter to the prime minister.
3 Kate .... got a houseboat in Bristol.
4 Mike and Sue .... her last weekend.

Negative sentences   weren't   doesn't   haven't   didn't

1 We .... got any money.
2 Mel .... like peas.
3 Ben .... go out last night.
4 Mike and Sue .... at home yesterday.

Questions   Have   Does   Are   Did

1 .... you having lunch in the canteen today?
2 .... Mike and Sue got our phone number?
3 .... Mel sing well last Saturday?
4 .... Ben go skateboarding every day?

How's it going?

● Your rating

Look again at pages 88–89. For each section give yourself a star rating:
Good ☆ ☆ ☆   Not bad ☆ ☆   I can't remember much ☆

● Vocabulary

Choose six words from the Vocabulary list and write six sentences: two affirmative, two negative and two questions.

● Test a friend

Look again at Units 7 and 8. Think of at least two questions, then ask a friend.

How old is the Earth?   Who's Richie Sowa?

● Correcting mistakes

Can you correct these mistakes?

1 I'm more taller than you.
2 It's the biggest plane of the world.
3 My computer is so powerful as Ben's.

● Your Workbook

Complete the Learning Diaries for Units 7 and 8.

Coursework 4 — My window on the world

Look at Matt's map, then draw a map of your country and write about 'superlative' places there.

Superlative places!

Hi! Here's my map of 'superlative Britain'. It shows some of the famous places here.

The wettest place in Britain is Cumbria, but it's also one of the most beautiful.

The highest mountain is Ben Nevis in Scotland. It's 1,342 metres high.

The coldest place is Braemar in Scotland. The average temperature is 6.5°C.

The second biggest city is Birmingham.

The longest river is the River Severn. It's 354 kilometres long.

The village with the longest name is Llanfairpwllgwyngyllgogerychwyrndrobwllllantysiliogogogoch, in Wales.

The warmest place is the Scilly Isles.

The biggest city in Britain is London.

The largest castle is Windsor Castle.

Module 5

A healthy future

In Module 5 you study

Grammar

- The future with *will/won't*
- Present continuous used for the future
- Countable and uncountable nouns
- Polite requests and offers
- *How much ... ? / How many ... ?*
- *A lot of / much / many*

Vocabulary

- Important events
- Future time expressions
- Food and drink

so that you can

- Talk about events in the future
- Ask and answer questions about the future
- Talk about future arrangements
- Ask politely for food and drink
- Offer other people food and drink
- Ask and answer questions about quantity
- Talk about different lifestyles
- Write about your lifestyle

Swim!

Chapter 3 – Emily's rival
Chapter 4 – A lot of money?

Life and culture

A basketball star
Would you like some waffles?

Coursework 5

On holiday!
You write about holidays in your country.

On holiday!

Hi! In this newsletter I'm going to tell you about my school holidays.

British schoolchildren usually have two weeks' holiday at Christmas, two weeks at Easter and about six weeks in the summer.

At Christmas we always have a Christmas tree, and presents, and everyone eats too much. We have turkey with roast potatoes and vegetables, and then Christmas pudding. Sometimes my grandparents come and stay with us. If it snows, I go tobogganing in the park. Manchester always looks beautiful, with lots of special lights.

At Easter, I sometimes go to Alton Towers theme park with my friends. We go on the coach and take a picnic lunch. My favourite ride

What's it about?

What can you say about the pictures?

Now match the pictures with sentences 1–5.

1 What will the future bring?
2 Can I speak to Natalie?
3 Would you like a drink?
4 How much blood have we got?
5 There's a banana tree in our garden.

Clara
Fortune Teller

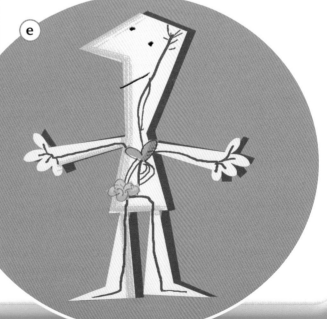

9 Looking ahead

STEP 1

In Step 1 you study
- the future with *will/won't*

so that you can
- talk about events in the future.

1 Reading *The luck factor*

a ⏱ Read the text. What's Dr Wiseman's message? You've got two minutes!

a Be optimistic!   b Everyone is lucky.
c You can't change your life.

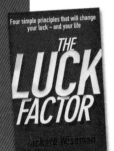

Four simple principles that will change your luck – and your life

THE LUCK FACTOR

Richard Wiseman

NO ONE KNOWS what will happen in the future, and life isn't always easy. But the psychologist Dr Richard Wiseman believes that we can all learn to be happier – if we have a positive attitude. Dr Wiseman and his team interviewed a thousand 'lucky' and 'unlucky' people. He found that unlucky people often have a pessimistic attitude towards life. Lucky people usually have an optimistic attitude. They look at the good things in their lives. When things go wrong, they try to learn from their mistakes. Dr Wiseman calls this attitude 'the luck factor'. He says it is the key to a happy life – and everyone can learn how to use it!

b Make two lists with these words.

pessimistic   lucky   sad   difficult   bad   right

Positive	Negative
lucky	pessimistic

Read the text again and find the opposites of the words in your lists.

optimistic   pessimistic

c If you have time, talk about your attitude. Are you an optimist or a pessimist? Share your ideas with your friends.

2 Presentation *You'll love it!*

a Look at the messages for Mel's article. Who are they from? Who are they for?

Mel is writing the September edition of the Westover School Magazine. She's choosing messages for her article.

Westover School Magazine
September
A WARM WELCOME
TO ALL OUR NEW STUDENTS
Good luck! You'll love it,
and the time will fly.
Rachel Field Class 8W

b 🔊 Listen to the messages and follow in your book. Who is optimistic and who is pessimistic?

c Imagine you're talking to a new student. Which messages are true for your school? Say the sentences.

3 Key grammar *will/won't*

a Which words show that the sentences are about the future?

b Complete the explanation.

I		
You	'll	have a great time.
He/She		
We	won't	like the food.
They		

The short form of will *is* _____ .
The short form of will not *is* _____ .

We use will/won't *when we talk about the* _____ .

G ➔ 7a, c

1 *Welcome to Westover! You'll have a great time.*
Claire Robbins Class 8B

2 *The older students will help you, so don't worry!*
Daniel Stoppard Class 8W

3 *You won't like the food in the canteen, and the toilets are awful.*
Megan Johns Class 8Y

4 *Everything will be fine. You'll make lots of new friends.*
Zak Green Class 8Y

5 *You won't be good at everything, but it won't be a problem. Just do your best.*
Tim Reeves Class 8B

6 *The school is very big. You'll probably get lost.*
Kim Taylor Class 8W

7 *Good luck! You'll love it and the time will fly.*
Rachel Field Class 8W

4 Practice

a Complete the sentences with *'ll* or *won't*.

1 The teachers are nice. You ....**'ll**.... like them.
2 Everyone's very friendly. We .... have a great time.
3 Don't worry! The work .... be too difficult.
4 You .... be in the same class as Paul. He .... be in Class 7Y and you .... be in Class 7H.
5 Are you nervous? I .... meet you at the school gate.
6 I .... be there at 8.30. I .... forget.

b Imagine your favourite star in 50 years' time. What will he/she be like? Make at least three sentences and share your ideas.

He'll be 75 years old. He won't be …

He'll have … He'll probably …

5 Speaking

Match the sentences with the pictures. Then work with a friend and practise the four conversations.

1 No, it won't. It's really friendly.
2 Don't worry! You'll be fine.
3 Of course you will! It'll be easy.
4 You never know! Ask her!

a I won't be happy here.

b I won't win.

c It'll bite me.

d She'll say 'No'.

6 Writing *My predictions*

Use what you know

Write at least three things for a friend who is starting at your school next term. Be positive!

You'll probably be nervous at first, but don't worry.

In Step 2 you study
- names of important events
- *will*: questions and short answers

so that you can
- ask and answer questions about the future

1 Key vocabulary
Important events

Match the words with the pictures.

1 take exams

get married	leave school
fall in love	take exams
pass exams	fail exams
go abroad	get a job
go out with someone	

🔊 Listen and check.

2 Presentation *What will happen?*

a Look at the photo. Is Matt talking about the past, the present or the future?

1 Will my brother pass his history exam?

2 Will I win the race next Saturday?

3 Will we walk on Mars one day?

4 What sort of job will I get?

5 Where will I live?

6 Will Natalie Price go out with me?

Clara
Fortune Teller
"What will the future bring?"

b 🔊 Close your book and listen to Matt's questions. What does he ask about – how many things can you remember?

c Match Matt's questions with these answers.

a You'll work with animals, I think.
b No, you won't. You'll be second.
c Perhaps she will. Perhaps she won't.
d Yes, he will.
e Probably. It'll happen one day.
f I don't know, but it won't be in a city.

🔊 Listen and check. Then ask and answer the questions.

3 Key grammar *Questions with* will

Complete the table.

Will	I/you/ he/she/ we/they	go abroad? win the race?
Yes, No,	I/you/he/ she/we/ they	....
Where	I/you/ he/she/ we/they	live? go?

G → 7b

4 Practice

a Put the words in the right order and make questions.

1 Will I be famous one day?

1 famous / be / I / day / will / one ?
2 pass / will / exam / Matt / his / maths ?
3 Sunday / Real Madrid / win / will / next ?
4 Tim / will / Sue / married / and / get / when ?
5 rain / it / tomorrow / will ?
6 school / will / leave / soon / you ?

b Think of answers for the questions in 4a, then ask and answer.

> Will Matt pass his maths exam?

> Yes, he will.

c **Test a friend** Write another question for 4a. Can your friend make the question?

be / tomorrow / it / hot / will ?

> Will it be hot tomorrow?

Try this!
Find six words from Exercise 1.

ELEVA AROBAD SAPS FILA SEMAX RAMDIRE

5 Key pronunciation /w/

Listen to the poem, then repeat it. Practise the 'w' sounds.

I want to be a wallaby,
A wallaby like Willoughby.
When *will* I be a wallaby
Like Willoughby the wallaby?

Colin West

6 Listening and speaking *Song*

a Listen to the song. Do we know what will happen to the man in the park?

b Complete the questions from the song.

1 Where .... he .... tonight?
2 Will he .... warm tonight?
3 What .... bring?

Listen and check.

c Share your ideas about the old man and the other people in the park.

> Will he be warm tonight?

> No, he won't. He'll be cold.

> He'll probably sleep under a bridge.

7 Writing and speaking *Questions about the future*

Use what you know

What do you want to know about the future? Write at least three questions, then work with a friend and act a short conversation with a fortune teller.

> Will I go abroad?   Yes, you will. You'll travel a lot.

In Step 3 you study
- future time expressions
- present continuous used for the future

so that you can
- talk about future arrangements

1 Key vocabulary *Future time expressions*

a How do you say these time expressions in your language?

at the weekend   next month   next summer
next week   next year   on Sunday   tonight
this evening   tomorrow   in August
tomorrow night   tomorrow morning

b Put the time expressions in order, starting with *this evening*.

🔲 Listen and check.

2 Presentation *She's going out this evening*

a 🔲 Close your book and listen to the telephone conversation. When is Natalie free?

Matt wants to speak to Natalie Price. He's talking to her sister.

MATT: Can I speak to Natalie, please?

LAURA: Sorry, but she isn't in. This is her sister.

MATT: Will she be in this evening?

LAURA: No. She's going out this evening. She's going to the cinema.

MATT: Oh. Er, will she be in tomorrow night?

LAURA: No, she won't. She's babysitting tomorrow. And we're playing tennis on Friday.

MATT: Oh.

LAURA: She'll be here on Saturday morning. Who's calling?

MATT: Oh, it doesn't matter. Thanks, anyway. Goodbye.

b 🔲 Listen again and follow in your book. Then ask and answer the questions.

1 Where's Natalie going this evening?
2 What's she doing tomorrow?
3 When's she playing tennis?
4 Is Natalie going out on Saturday morning?

3 Key grammar
Present continuous used for the future

Complete the explanation.

I'm/You're/ He's/She's/ We're/They're	babysitting playing tennis	tomorrow. on Friday.
Are you/Is she	going out	this evening?

We use the .... tense + a future time expression to describe arrangements for the future.

G ➔ 5d

4 Practice

Write sentences. Use these time expressions.

tomorrow night   on Saturday   in July
at the weekend   next summer   tomorrow morning

1 Natalie's having a party at the weekend.

1 Natalie / have a party
2 I / get up early
3 Ben / babysit
4 We / go to Spain
5 Mel / play hockey
6 My friend / come here

5 Speaking

a Match the sentences and make two conversations.

1 I'm going to a basketball match on Saturday.
2 I'm not doing anything tomorrow.

a Well, why don't you come to my house?
b That's nice.

b What about you? Talk about your future arrangements.

6 Writing and speaking
A telephone conversation

Use what you know

Work with a friend. Write a conversation like the one between Matt and Laura. Change some of the details.

Swim!

Emily's rival

The next morning, Emily's alarm clock rang at six o'clock. She jumped out of bed and quickly put her swimming things into her bag. She went downstairs quietly. She took a banana from the kitchen for breakfast.

'Where are you going?' Emily was walking out of the door when she heard her father's voice.

'The pool,' she answered.

'What, so early?'

'I'll tell you about it later, Dad,' said Emily. She ran out of the house.

At the pool, she watched the other swimmers for a few minutes. She noticed a woman in a blue swimsuit. The woman was swimming very fast.

'Is that Tina Dawson?' she asked Jack.

'Yes, it is.'

Emily looked at Dawson, moving through the water. 'She's good, very good!' she said.

'Yes, she wants to win the Picton Lake Race for the fifth time,' Jack replied. 'But don't think about her. Come on, get in the water! Swim!'

Emily's training session finished at 8.30. Then she got on the bus to go to school. 'Only three more weeks before the summer holiday,' she thought. On the bus, the man next to her was reading 'The Picton News'. She read the headline.

'Businessman offers £50,000 to winner of Picton Lake Race.'

'Wow!' thought Emily. '£50,000 is a lot of money!' But how was she going to beat someone like Tina Dawson?

Questions

1 Why did Emily get up early?
2 Why is Tina Dawson training at the pool?
3 What will the winner of the race get?

Extra exercises

1 Choose the right words.

1 They fell .... love when they met in Spain.
   - a in
   - b to
   - c for

2 I think I'll .... the exam. It wasn't very difficult.
   - a pass
   - b fail
   - c take

3 Bill will come with Angela He's .... with her now.
   - a coming in
   - b coming out
   - c going out

4 Susan decided to .... school when she was sixteen.
   - a study
   - b go
   - c leave

5 They aren't going .... in the summer. They're staying here.
   - a above
   - b along
   - c abroad

6 Eva and George .... married two months ago.
   - a went
   - b got
   - c did

2 Complete the sentences with 'll, will or won't.

1 Robert hasn't got a map. I think he .... get lost.

2 You .... like that book. It's boring.

3 Don't worry about your driving test. Everything .... be fine.

4 Carla .... have any chicken. She's a vegetarian.

5 It's a very strange story. I don't think people .... believe it.

6 I .... get a phone call from my parents soon.

3 Complete the questions. Use will + ...

1 A: .... Steve tomorrow?
   B: No, I don't think I'll see him before Thursday.

2 A: .... married next year?
   B: Yes, I'm sure they will.

3 A: What do you think? .... at Nick's party?
   B: No, she won't be there.

4 A: When .... ? Do you know?
   B: I'm not sure, but I think he'll arrive at about eight o'clock.

5 A: Where .... in the summer?
   B: They'll probably stay with their grandparents.

6 A: Which subjects .... at university?
   B: I don't know. Maybe I'll study languages.

4 Read the text and choose the right word for each space.

It's Friday, but Graham isn't going out [1].......... evening because he's got a lot of things to do [2].......... the weekend. He's going to the sports club [3].......... morning and then he's meeting Luke for lunch. There's a band practice tomorrow [4].......... at 2.30 – it's really important because they're playing at the school concert next [5].......... . On [6].......... Graham has got a ticket for Manchester United. On Sunday evening, he's staying [7].......... home. He needs to study because his exams are starting [8].......... month.

1 a on	b in	c this
2 a in	b at	c for
3 a tomorrow	b next	c in
4 a afternoon	b evening	c night
5 a day	b week	c tomorrow
6 a evening	b September	c Sunday
7 a at	b to	c in
8 a next	b in	c last

5 Match the sentences in A with the sentences in B.

A	B
1 We've got our tickets.	a I'm starting on Monday.
2 I got an email from Liz.	b We aren't playing on Saturday.
3 I've got a new job.	c I'm not cooking tonight.
4 I can't see you in the morning.	d We're getting the 9.30 train.
5 We aren't in the team.	e I'm going to the doctor.
6 There's a pizza in the fridge.	f She's meeting us after lunch.

6 How do you say these sentences in your language?

1 Do your best.
2 The time will fly.
3 Don't worry! You'll be fine.
4 You never know.
5 She isn't in.
6 Who's calling?
7 It doesn't matter.
8 I can't come, anyway.

Extra reading

A basketball star

Do you play basketball? What's your favourite sport?

When Rocky Wood was at primary school, a local newspaper called him 'the best primary school player in the city'. Now, at the age of 15, he plays in one of the best high school teams in Chicago. In their last game Rocky scored 39 points!

He lives in a small apartment in a Chicago suburb with his mother, father, younger brother and two sisters. His family is not rich but Rocky hopes that, one day, he will change that. If he becomes a basketball star, they'll move to a bigger and better apartment. 'And my mom and dad won't need to work so hard,' he says.

Basketball is Rocky's life. He practises every day. At the weekends he runs to the top of his apartment building – and there are fourteen floors. Even more incredible, he does it three times!

Rocky told us, 'When I was in junior high school, I played other sports and went to the movies. But now basketball is like a full-time job.'

ABOUT BASKETBALL

A lot of famous players are very tall. Michael Jordan, who played for the Chicago Bulls, is 1.98 m, and Magic Johnson from the Los Angeles Lakers is 2.06 m tall. At 2.34 m, Gheorghe Muresan from Romania is probably the tallest player in the world. But smaller players are often the fastest!

Task

Read the text, then answer these questions.

1 Is Rocky at primary school?
2 Why was he in the newspapers?
3 Did he play well in his last game?
4 Does Rocky live in the city centre?
5 Has his family got much money?
6 Why does he want to move?
7 Does he have much free time?

10 Some ketchup, please!

STEP 1

In Step 1 you study

- names of food and drink
- uncountable nouns
- *I'd like a/some ... ; Would you like a/some ... ? ; Could I have a/some ... ?*

so that you can

- ask politely for food and drink
- offer other people food and drink

1 Key vocabulary *Food and drink*

a 🕐 Match the words with the pictures. You've got three minutes!

beefburger   baked potato   biscuits
salad   peas   sauce   sausages   rice
soup   grapes   sugar   mineral water

🔊 Listen and check.

b What about you? In your opinion, what are the three nicest things in the list?

baked potato, grapes ...

2 Presentation *Would you like some sauce?*

a What can you say about the photo?

b 🔊 Close your book and listen to the conversation. How many 'food and drink' words can you hear?

The Kellys are having a barbecue in their garden. Jack and his mother, Sally, are there.

MR KELLY: Jack, would you like a beefburger, a veggieburger or some sausages?

JACK: Er, could I have a beefburger and some sausages?

MR KELLY: Yes, sure. Would you like some 'special Caribbean barbecue sauce'?

JACK: No, thanks. I think I'll have some ketchup.

MR KELLY: What about you, Sally?

MRS ELLIS: I'd like a veggieburger and a baked potato, please, Mike. And I'd like some barbecue sauce, please.

MR KELLY: OK.

SADIE: Would you like a drink, Sally?

MRS ELLIS: Yes, please.

SADIE: Lemonade or fruit juice?

MRS ELLIS: Could I have some lemonade?

SADIE: Here you are. Help yourself to some salad.

MRS ELLIS: Thanks very much.

c Listen again and follow in your book. Are these sentences true or false? Correct the false sentences.

1. Jack isn't very hungry.
2. Jack doesn't want any ketchup.
3. Sally isn't having any sausages.
4. The Kellys haven't got any fruit juice.
5. Sally would like some lemonade.
6. There isn't any salad.

3 Key grammar I'd like + a/some; Could I have + a/some ... ?

a Complete the explanation.

Countable nouns		Uncountable nouns
Singular	*Plural*	
beefburger	peas	sauce
potato	sausages	salad
Have **a** beefburger. There are **some** sausages.		There's **some** salad.

We use _____ *with singular nouns, and* _____ *with plural nouns and uncountable nouns.*

G▶ 18a-c, 19a-c

b How do you say these 'polite sentences' in your language?

I'd like some salad, please. (I'd = I would)
Would you like a drink?
Could I have some soup?

G▶ 15a-b

4 Practice

a Complete the sentences with *a* or *some*.

1. There are _____ grapes in the fridge.
2. Sadie's having _____ veggieburger and _____ salad.
3. Her gran wants _____ cup of tea and _____ biscuits.
4. I'll have _____ fruit juice, please.
5. Would you like _____ peas?
6. Could I have _____ sugar, please?
7. There's _____ bottle of ketchup in the cupboard.
8. I'd like _____ water, please.

b Test a friend Write another sentence for 4a. Leave a space for *a* or *some*. Can your friend complete the sentence?

Would you like _____ *rice?*

5 Key pronunciation *Weak forms*

 Listen and repeat the sentences. Practise the /ə/ sound in *some, a, of, and.*

1. Some peas, please.
2. A cup of coffee, please.
3. A glass of water, please.
4. Steak and chips, please.

6 Speaking

a Work with a friend. Complete the conversation with these words.

a cheese and tomato sandwich   a drink
some apple juice

A: Would you like _____ ?
B: Yes, please. Could I have _____ ?
A: What would you like to eat?
B: I'd like _____ , please.

b Make a different conversation. Change what B says.

7 Listening
The school canteen

It's lunchtime. Jack, Sadie, Lisa and Ben are in the queue in the school canteen.

a Look at the list of food, then listen to the conversation. There's one thing that isn't on the list. What is it?

1. baked beans   2. baked potato
3. cheese   4. chicken   5. chips
6. pasta   7. peas   8. salad
9. veggieburger

b Listen again. What's everyone having? Write the names and the right numbers. *Jack 4, 7*

8 Writing and speaking *Lunchtime*

Use what you know

Imagine you're having lunch in the canteen at Westover School. Work in a group and write a conversation. Then act your conversation.

What would you like?
Could I have a baked potato?
Would you like some bread?

In Step 2 you study
- *How much ... ? / How many ... ?*

so that you can
- ask and answer questions about quantity

The quantity quiz

1 Presentation
How much blood have you got?

a Read the quiz. Check the words you don't understand.

b 🕐 Write the answers. If you don't know, guess. You've got five minutes! *1c*

c 📻 Listen to the questions and answers. How many right answers have you got?

2 Key grammar *How much/many?*

Complete the table with *much* and *many*. Then complete the explanation.

How	_____	water is there?
		sleep do you get?
	_____	biscuits do you eat?
		elephants are there?

We use _____ with uncountable nouns and _____ with plural nouns.

G ➔ 20b-c

3 Practice

Complete the sentences.

1 How _____ orange juice is there?
2 How _____ chairs are there?
3 How _____ sandwiches have you got?
4 How _____ bread have we got?
5 How much paper _____ there?
6 How many people _____ there?

Try this!
How many words do you know for parts of the body? Write a list.
teeth, brain

---

1 How much water does an elephant drink?
  a Between 25 and 30 litres a day.
  b About 50 litres a day.
  c Between 80 and 160 litres a day.

2 How many 'cookies' does the average North American eat?
  a 350 a year.
  b About 500 a year.
  c More than 1,000 a year.

3 How much blood is there in our bodies?
  a About three litres.
  b Between four and five litres.
  c About six litres.

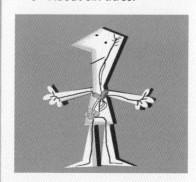

4 How many times a day do we blink?
  a About 9,000.
  b About 12,000.
  c About 15,000.

4 Writing and speaking

a Make questions with *How much/many* for these answers.

  1 How much fish do the Japanese eat?

1 The Japanese eat <u>25,000 tons of fish</u> a year.
2 There are <u>a thousand metres</u> in a kilometre.
3 About <u>400,000 babies</u> are born every day.
4 An African elephant weighs <u>five tons</u>.
5 The Chinese eat <u>365,000 tons of rice</u> a day.
6 A jumbo jet can carry more than <u>500 people</u>.

5 How many teeth has an adult got?
a 28   b 30   c 32

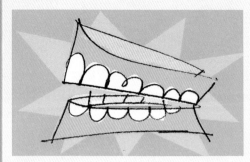

6 How much sleep does an average adult get?
a   About six hours a night.
b   About seven hours a night.
c   About eight hours a night.

7 How much does your brain weigh?
a   About 500 grams.
b   1.4 kilos.
c   About two kilos.

b Work with a friend. Ask and answer the questions.

c If you have time, make another question with *How much/many* and ask a friend.

5 Reading   *An average person in the USA.*

a Read about Michael Smith. What is the text based on?

a   an interview with Michael   b   a survey of life in the USA
c   Michael's diary

Michael Smith was born at four minutes past five this morning in an average hospital in an average American town. We already know quite a lot about him.

In his lifetime, Michael will eat approximately 30 tons of food, and he'll use 28 million litres of water. He'll spend four hours a day in front of the TV, and 2.5 hours a day in his car. He'll spend 40 minutes a week playing with his children. He'll have at least 13 credit cards and he'll make more than a thousand phone calls every year. He'll probably have four or five different jobs. He'll get married at the age of 26 and he'll die at the age of 77.

b Read the text again. Write the answer or 'We don't know' for these questions.

1 30 tons.

1   How much food will Michael eat?
2   How much water will he drink?
3   Will he watch a lot of TV?
4   Will he drive to work?
5   Will he spend much time with his children?
6   How much money will he have?
7   Will he have the same job all his life?

6 Writing and speaking   *Questions about quantity*

Use what you know

Think of more questions for a 'quantity quiz'.
Use *How much/many*. Here are some ideas.

minutes / an hour   money / a millionaire
tomato ketchup / the British   people / a football team

Share your ideas and make a list of questions on the board. How many questions can you answer?

In Step 3 you study
- *a lot of / much / many*

so that you can
- talk about different lifestyles
- write about your lifestyle

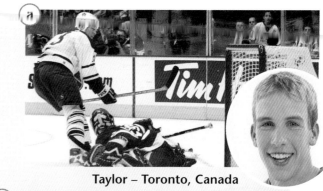

Taylor – Toronto, Canada

1 Presentation *There isn't much fresh air*

a Match the texts with the photos.

We asked three teenagers 'Have you got a healthy lifestyle?'

1 'We live in the middle of the city and the air's very polluted here. I don't spend much time outside, and I don't get much exercise. I suppose it isn't a very healthy lifestyle.'

2 'Me and my friends are crazy about ice hockey! We all do a lot of sport. But we eat a lot of fast food, and we don't have many fresh vegetables. I don't really know if my lifestyle is healthy or unhealthy.'

3 'My dad's a fisherman, so we eat a lot of fish. There's a banana tree in our garden, so we have a lot of bananas too. There aren't many cars here, so we usually play outside. We haven't got much money, but everyone in my family seems happy and healthy!'

Harriet – St. John's, Antigua

Listen and check your answers.

b Match the words in A with the words in B, then ask and answer the questions.

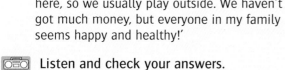

> 1 Does Yannis do much sport?   No, he doesn't.

A		B
1	Does Yannis do much	a cars in Athens?
2	Does he get much	b vegetables?
3	Are there many	c sport?
4	Does Taylor go to many	d fruit?
5	Does he eat many	e money?
6	Does Harriet eat much	f ice hockey matches?
7	Have her parents got much	g exercise?

Yannis – Athens, Greece

2 Key grammar *a lot of / much / many*

Read the explanation and complete the examples with *much* or *many*.

> We usually use much and many *in negative sentences and in questions.*
>
> There aren't many cars.   Has he got _____ friends?
> There isn't _____ fresh air.   Have they got _____ money?
>
> We usually use a lot of *in affirmative sentences, but we can use it in negative sentences and questions too.*

 20a–c

3 Practice

Complete the sentences with *much* or *many*.

1 Yannis doesn't get _____ fresh air.
2 Are there _____ restaurants in your town?
3 Hurry up! We haven't got _____ time.
4 Do you watch _____ television?
5 There aren't _____ buses on Sunday.
6 Were there _____ people at the party?
7 Do you do _____ sport?
8 I don't eat _____ biscuits.

4 Writing *My lifestyle*

Use what you know

Write at least four sentences about your lifestyle. Make two lists.

Healthy   *I eat a lot of fruit.*
Unhealthy   *I don't get much exercise.*

Swim!

A lot of money

For the next few weeks Emily just thought about Jack's voice saying 'Swim!' Every morning before school, she swam. She wanted to win the race and beat Tina Dawson.

One morning, Tina Dawson watched Emily swimming. Dawson started talking to Jack Hastings.

'What's her name?' she asked.

'Emily James,' Jack replied.

'She's a good swimmer,' she said.

'Yes,' said Jack, 'she is. Excellent.'

'So you must be a good trainer …' said Dawson.

'Well, I …'

'Oh come on,' said the former champion. 'I watch you, I watch her. She gets better every day. You're the best.'

Jack looked at Tina Dawson.

'Do you want to make a lot of money?' she continued. 'I mean, if you work with me …'

Jack decided that he didn't like Dawson.

'I mean, work with me, not her.'

Now he really disliked Tina Dawson.

'You could make some money,' she said, 'some real money. If I win this race, I'll get £50,000.'

'I'm sorry, Miss Dawson,' Jack said, moving away from her. 'I'm training Emily, money or no money.'

Jack walked away from Dawson and towards Emily, who was just finishing her swim. Dawson looked at them. She wasn't smiling. She was angry now.

'Well, there are other ways,' Dawson thought, 'of stopping Emily James!'

Questions

1 Why did Tina Dawson notice Emily?
2 What did Dawson offer Jack? Why?
3 Did Jack accept her offer? Why not?

Extra exercises

1 Choose the right words.

1 _____ I have some bread, please?
   a Will
   b Would
   c Could

2 _____ like an orange, please.
   a I
   b I'd
   c Could I

3 What _____ like to eat?
   a you
   b you'd
   c would you

4 How _____ do our bags weigh?
   a much
   b many
   c heavy

5 She bought half a kilo _____ .
   a sugar
   b of sugar
   c of sugars

6 Let's get _____ fresh air.
   a a
   b an
   c some

2 Which word is the odd one out?

1 salad

1 beefburger salad chicken sausage
2 grapes peas beans potatoes
3 lemonade ketchup juice water
4 cheese butter rice yoghurt
5 bread cookie biscuit soup
6 gram kilo metre ton

3 Complete the questions with *much* or *many*.

1 How _____ potatoes do you want?
2 Have we got _____ time?
3 Do you eat _____ rice?
4 How _____ milk do we need?
5 Did you spend _____ money?
6 How _____ people were at the match?

4 Match the answers with the questions in Exercise 3.

a Two litres.
b No, I don't like it.
c About 30,000.
d Just one, please.
e Yes, it's OK. We've got an hour.
f No, I didn't.

5 Complete the sentences with *much* or *many*.

1 There aren't _____ good programmes on TV this week.
2 You don't get _____ exercise. Why don't you come to the gym with me?
3 Do _____ students play ice hockey?
4 Is there _____ pasta in the cupboard?
5 Have _____ people in your class got a mobile phone?
6 I don't eat _____ fish.

6 Complete the conversations.

1 Would you like some _____
   a grape?
   b bread?
   c pea?

2 Could I _____
   a have a drink?
   b some fruit juice?
   c a biscuit, please?

3 I'd like a _____
   a rice, please.
   b kilo, please.
   c potatoes, please.

4 What would you like _____
   a eat?
   b drink?
   c to eat?

7 How do you say these sentences in your language?

1 Help yourself.
2 What would you like to eat?
3 Could I have some water, please?
4 We're crazy about ice hockey.
5 I fancy the pasta.
6 We know quite a lot about him.

Would you like some waffles?

**What do you know about food in the USA?
Do you eat any 'American' food?**

Meals and meal times

Breakfast People in the USA eat when they wake up. Traditionally, people eat: eggs, bacon, toast, bagels, cereal, donuts, waffles, pancakes, yoghurt or fruit. They drink milk, juice, tea or coffee. But sometimes young people today have a 'candy bar' and a coke for their breakfast!

Lunch Between 11am and 2pm. People usually have sandwiches, soup, fries, salad, fruit, cookies. They drink juice, milk or soda. Schools often serve hot and cold lunches.

Dinner Between 4.30pm and 7.30pm. Hot meals include: steak, potatoes, vegetables, noodles, chicken, fish or roast meat. A lot of families eat a 'TV dinner' in front of the television — frozen meals and pizza are popular. But many families don't often eat dinner together, because everyone is too busy. Eating at a restaurant is also quite common.

Martha's Bar

Starters	
Pumpkin soup	3.00
California dip *(Onions and sour cream)*	3.50
Tex-Mex Dip *(Avocados, sour cream, beans, olives, tomatoes and onions)*	4.25
Main dishes	
Burger and fries	5.95
Macaroni and cheese	6.50
New England boiled dinner *(Beef and vegetables)*	8.50
Boston baked beans *(Beans with pork)*	7.95
Side dishes	
Fried green tomatoes	1.50
Glazed carrots	0.95
Spanish rice	2.25
Hashed brown potatoes	2.25
Salads	
Three-bean salad	1.75
Potato salad	1.50
Desserts	
Apple pie and cream	2.95
German chocolate cake	3.75
Pineapple upside-down cake	3.75

ABOUT FOOD IN THE USA

A lot of the early American immigrants died because they didn't have enough to eat. Today, many Americans die because they eat too much.

Task

1 Look at the information about meals and mealtimes in the USA. Find at least three differences between the USA and your country.

2 Look at the menu from an American restaurant and choose your meal. What would you like?

Module 5 Review

Language summary

1 The future with *will*

We use *will* + verb to talk about the future.

Affirmative and negative

I/You/ He/She/It	'll	be there tomorrow.
We/You/ They	won't	be late.

Questions and short answers

Will	I/you/he/she/it/ we/you/they	win the race?
Yes, No,	I/you/he/she/it/ we/they	will. won't.
'll = will won't = will not		

Check that you can

1.1 ● describe future events.

Complete the sentences with *'ll, will* or *won't* and these verbs.

not remember   pass   help
not be   win   not need   get

1 I'm sure Joe <u>will help</u> you. He's good at maths.
2 Lisa _____ . She's got an awful memory.
3 I think Juventus _____ the next European Cup. They're brilliant.
4 Matt isn't sure but they _____ probably _____ the ferry.
5 I can't find my jacket. My mother _____ very pleased.
6 Jack isn't very optimistic. He doesn't think he _____ all his exams.
7 It's hot today. You _____ a coat.

1.2 ● ask and answer questions about the future.

Complete the questions in A, then match them with the answers in B. Ask and answer.

> Will you be in this evening?

> Yes, I will.

A
1 _____ you be in this evening?
2 _____ it rain this afternoon?
3 _____ Matt be pleased?
4 _____ Lisa like her present?
5 _____ Sue and Mike go abroad?
6 _____ I get the right answers?

B
a No, they _____ .
b No, it _____ .
c Yes, she _____ .
d No, he _____ .
e Yes, I _____ .
f Yes, of course you _____ !

2 Present continuous used for the future

We use the present continuous to talk about definite arrangements for the future.

> I'm meeting Danny outside the café.
> Lisa's having a party next weekend.
> Karen and Colin are getting married in October.

Check that you can

● talk about arrangements for the future.

Respond to the questions with: *Sorry, but I'm ... with Natalie ... .*

1 *Sorry, but I'm having a pizza with Natalie after school.*
1 Shall we have a pizza after school?
2 Do you want to go swimming tomorrow?
3 Why don't we watch a video this evening?
4 Shall we walk home together?
5 Shall we go to the cinema on Friday?
6 Let's go bowling on Saturday.

3 Countable and uncountable nouns

In English, nouns can be 'countable' (things you can count) or 'uncountable' (things you can't count).

Countable nouns: singular

a sock

an apple

a frog

Countable nouns: plural

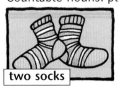
two socks

some apples

five frogs

Uncountable nouns

bread

music

water

Uncountable nouns are always singular. We cannot say ~~some breads~~. But we don't use *a/an* with them, we use *some* or *any*.

*We've got **some** sugar.*
*Is there **any** butter?*

Some nouns can be countable or uncountable:

singular	uncountable	plural
	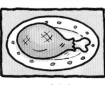	
a chicken	**some chicken**	**some chickens**

Check that you can

- use countable and uncountable nouns.

Write the names of each item. Use *a/an* or *some*.

1 some sugar

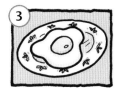

4 *some* and *any*

We usually use:

- *some* in affirmative sentences:
  There's some salad and there are some sandwiches.

- *any* in negative sentences:
  There isn't any salad and there aren't any sandwiches.

- *any* in questions like these:
  Is there any salad? Are there any sandwiches?
  Have you got any ketchup?

Check that you can

- use *some* and *any*.

Complete the sentences with *some* or *any*.

1 Lee can't come. He hasn't got _____ money.
2 I want to write a letter. Is there _____ paper?
3 I'd like _____ chips but I don't want _____ peas.
4 Are you hungry? There's _____ chicken in the fridge.
5 Do you know _____ famous athletes?
6 Is there _____ brown bread?
7 I haven't got _____ football boots. Can I borrow yours?
8 I won't have _____ pasta, thanks.

5 Would you like ... ? Could I have ... ?

In polite offers and requests, we use *a/an/some* – we don't use *any*.

> Would you like **a** glass of wine?
> Could I have **an** orange?
> Would you like **some** bread?
> Could I have **some** biscuits?

Check that you can

- offer things and ask for things politely.

Complete the sentences with *a, an* or *some*.

1 Could I have _____ omelette, please?
2 Would you like _____ chicken soup?
3 Could we have _____ table by the window?
4 Could I have _____ chips, please?
5 Would you like _____ ice in your drink?
6 Would you like _____ telescope for your birthday?

6 *a lot of/much/many*

We use *a lot of* with countable and uncountable nouns. We use *much* with uncountable nouns and *many* with countable nouns.

Uncountable nouns	Plural nouns
Ben's got **a lot of** pasta.	Lisa's got **a lot of** sausages.
There isn't **much** sugar.	There aren't **many** biscuits.
Is there **much** paper?	Are there **many** cars?

A lot of and lots of *have the same meaning. We can use* a lot of/lots of *in negatives and questions.*

Check that you can

- use *much* and *many*.

These sentences are wrong. Write the opposite. Use *much* or *many*.

1 That's not true! Sally hasn't got much money.

1 Jack's mum Sally has got lots of money.
2 There are a lot of skyscrapers in Exeter.
3 There are lots of trees in the Sahara Desert.
4 There are lots of people in Antarctica.
5 There's a lot of traffic there.
6 Joe and Sadie do a lot of housework.

Vocabulary

Important events
(to) fail exams
(to) fall in love
(to) get a job
(to) get married
(to) go abroad
(to) go out with (someone)
(to) leave school
(to) pass exams
(to) take exams

Future time expressions
at the weekend
in August
next month
next summer
next week
next year
on Sunday
this evening
tomorrow
tomorrow morning
tomorrow afternoon
tomorrow evening
tomorrow night
tonight

Food and drink
baked beans
baked potato
beefburger
biscuit
cheese
chicken
chips
coffee
cookies*
fish
fruit juice
grapes
lemonade
meat
mineral water
pasta
peas
rice
salad
sauce
sausage
soup
sugar
tea
veggieburger
vegetables

Expressions
Do your best.
Help yourself.
Here you are.
It doesn't matter.
She isn't in.
Thanks, anyway.
The time will fly.
They're crazy about ice hockey.
Will you be in this evening?

*American English

Study skills 5
Guessing what words mean

We can sometimes understand a new word because the other words in the sentences are 'clues'.

🕐 Read the sentences then look at the pictures. Choose the right word and complete the sentences. You've got five minutes!

snooker   climb   melt   dustbin   moon   storm

1 It's so hot! My ice cream is going to _____ .
2 Shall we play _____ ? There's a table in the games room.
3 I like astronomy. I'm interested in the _____ and the stars.
4 Edmund Hillary and Tensing Norgay were the first people to _____ Mount Everest.
5 I couldn't sleep last night. There was a really bad _____ .
6 These yoghurts are six weeks old! Put them in the _____ .

Which words are 'clues'?   1 hot

How's it going?

- ### Your rating

Look again at pages 110–111. For each section give yourself a star rating:
Good ☆☆☆   Not bad ☆☆   I can't remember much ☆

- ### Vocabulary

Look at the Vocabulary list. Which words are difficult to pronounce? Write the six most difficult words. Then work with a friend and compare your lists.

- ### Test a friend

Look again at Units 9 and 10. Think of at least two questions, then ask a friend.

> What is Richard Wiseman's job?
> How much water does an elephant drink?

- ### Correcting mistakes

Can you correct these mistakes?

1 ~~Could I have peanuts?~~
2 ~~He will win?~~
3 ~~How much people are there?~~

- ### Your Workbook

Complete the Learning Diaries for Units 9 and 10.

Coursework 5 **My window on the world**

Read Matt's newsletter, then write about holidays in your country.
Use pictures, photos and drawings.

On holiday!

Hi! In this newsletter I'm going to tell you about my school holidays.

British schoolchildren usually have two weeks' holiday at Christmas, two weeks at Easter and about six weeks in the summer.

At Christmas we always have a Christmas tree, and presents, and everyone eats too much. We have turkey with roast potatoes and vegetables, and then Christmas pudding. Sometimes my grandparents come and stay with us. If it snows, I go tobogganing in the park. Manchester always looks beautiful, with lots of special lights.

At Easter, I sometimes go to Alton Towers theme park with my friends. We go on the coach and take a picnic lunch. My favourite ride is the 'Black Hole' – it's a roller coaster in the dark. Last year we went on the new 'Spinball Whizzer' and everyone felt ill.

In the summer, we often go to France in our caravan. Sometimes I go to Jack's house in Exeter. I'm going to stay with him in August. We'll probably go camping on Dartmoor, so I hope the weather will be good.

Module 6

Looking back

In Module 6 you study

Grammar

- *Can/can't*
- *Must/mustn't*
- *Should/shouldn't*
- First conditional

Vocabulary

- Verbs of action
- Names of everyday materials

so that you can

- Talk about what is and isn't possible
- Talk about rules and obligations
- Understand advice and say if it is good or bad
- Talk about a problem and give your opinion
- Talk about recycling and the environment
- Learn about our changing climate
- Talk about results and consequences

Swim!

Chapter 5 – The big day
Chapter 6 – The winner

Life and culture

A letter from Canada
The World Wide Fund For Nature

Coursework 6

A visit to my country
You write about your country.

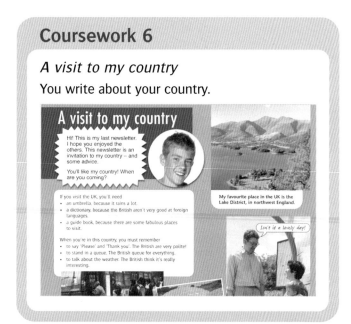

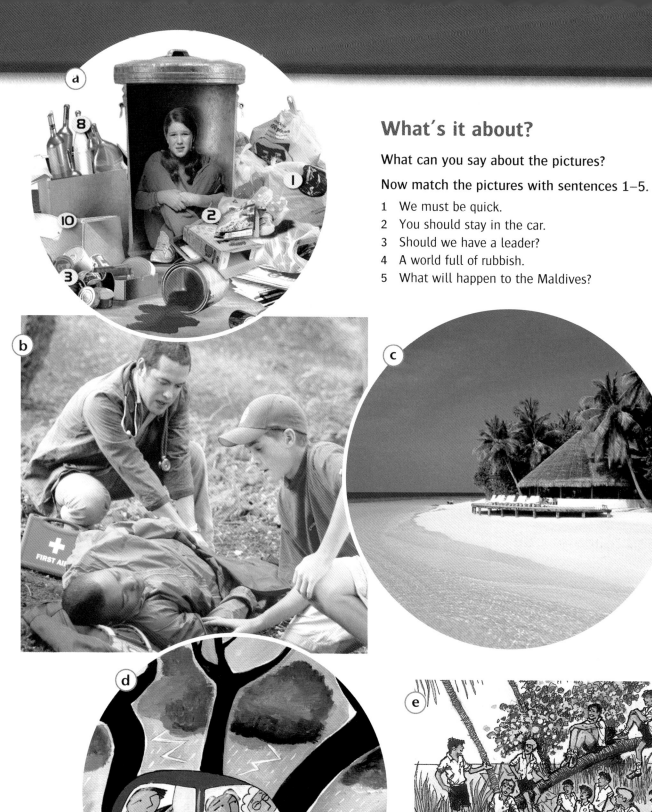

What's it about?

What can you say about the pictures?

Now match the pictures with sentences 1–5.

1 We must be quick.
2 You should stay in the car.
3 Should we have a leader?
4 A world full of rubbish.
5 What will happen to the Maldives?

11 In the wild

Ben Nevis
Edinburgh

STEP 1

In Step 1 you study
- can/can't
- must/mustn't

so that you can
- talk about what is and isn't possible
- talk about rules and obligations

1 Presentation *We mustn't panic!*

a 🔊 Listen to the story and follow in your book. Guess what will happen next.

Matt and his friend Wayne are staying at a Youth Hostel in Scotland. They're on Ben Nevis – the highest mountain in Britain.

> Wayne! Are you all right?

> No, I'm not. I can't move my leg. I think it's broken.

> Broken! OK! Rule number one: We mustn't panic.

> It really hurts. We must get some help, Matt.

> I'll go back to the hostel.

> Can you remember the way?

> 1 _____ I'll be as quick as I can.

> I haven't got much food.

> You can have mine. And take my jacket. You mustn't get cold.

> Thanks Matt.

Three hours later ...

> 2 _____ Look! He's down there.

> It isn't going to be easy. 3 _____

> Wayne, it's Matt. 4 _____

> Don't worry, Matt. He'll be OK. 5 _____

b Match these sentences with the numbers in the story.

- a Wayne, can you hear me?
- b I can see my red jacket!
- c But we must be quick.
- d Yes, of course I can.
- e We mustn't go too near those trees.

🔊 Listen again and check.

c Match the words in A with the words in B and make complete sentences.

A
1 Wayne can't walk
2 When you're in a difficult situation,
3 The people in the helicopter can see Wayne
4 The pilot must be careful
5 Wayne will be OK

B
a because there are lots of trees.
b but they must hurry.
c because he's got Matt's red jacket.
d because his leg is broken.
e you mustn't panic.

2 Key grammar can/can't; must/mustn't

Complete the explanation.

| I/He/She You/We/They | can see Wayne. can't move. |
| | must go. mustn't panic. |

We use _____ or _____ + verb when something is or isn't possible.
We use _____ or _____ + verb for rules and obligations.

Remember! We don't use to after can *and* must.

G ➤ 11a–b, 12

3 Practice

a Complete the sentences. Use *can, can't, must, mustn't.*

1 Can you hear anything? – No, I _____ .
2 It's dangerous. Matt _____ be careful.
3 They _____ walk there in ten minutes. It isn't far.
4 It's late. She _____ go to bed.
5 I _____ move my arm. I think it's broken.
6 _____ we stay at the Youth Hostel? – Yes, you can.
7 You _____ talk. Be quiet!
8 Ben wants to go skateboarding but he _____ find his skateboard.

b **Role play** If you have time, act the story. Work in a group of four: Matt, Wayne, the pilot and the doctor.

4 Reading and speaking *Notices*

a Read the notices. Find something that you like playing and something that you like eating.
🕐 You've got two minutes!

b Read the notices again, then say at least four things about the Youth Hostel. Use *can, can't, must, mustn't.*

> You mustn't smoke.

> You can have porridge for breakfast.

5 Writing and speaking *Our school*

Use what you know

Think about the things you can/can't do at your school, and the things you must/mustn't do. Write at least three sentences, then share your ideas.

At our school, you can play volleyball, but you can't play tennis.
You mustn't eat in the classrooms.

In Step 2 you study
- verbs of action
- *should/shouldn't*

so that you can
- understand advice and say if it is good or bad
- talk about a problem and give your opinion

1 Key vocabulary
Verbs of action

⏱ **Match the verbs with the pictures. You've got two minutes!**

run away   run after   climb   follow
move   touch   get into   get out of

🔈 Listen and check.

Answers

1. a No, you shouldn't! The poison from desert scorpions can be very dangerous.
2. b Not a very good idea. You can't be sure that someone will find you.
3. a Not a good idea. Bears can climb trees too.
4. b You shouldn't go outside when there's a storm.
5. c It'll probably run after you. You should walk.

2 Presentation   *You should be careful.*

a 🔈 **Listen to the quiz and follow in your book. What can you say about the pictures?**

b **Read the quiz again. Which sentences are bad advice? Write your answers, then check in the box.** *1a*

ARE YOU A SURVIVOR?

Do you know what to do when you're in danger? There are five pieces of 'bad' advice here. Can you find them?

1 You're in the Sahara Desert. There are a lot of scorpions.

a You should try them for your breakfast.
b You should look carefully before you get into your sleeping bag.
c You should check your clothes before you get dressed.

2 You're lost in the mountains. You haven't got a map.

a You should find a river, then follow it.
b You shouldn't move. Someone will find you.
c You shouldn't eat all your food immediately.

3 Key grammar   should/shouldn't

Complete the explanation.

| I/He/She | should be careful. |
| You/We/They | shouldn't shout. |

We use _____ or _____ + verb when we give advice.
Remember! We don't use to *after* should.

G ➜ 13a. c

Try this!
How many names of wild animals
do you know in English?
bear

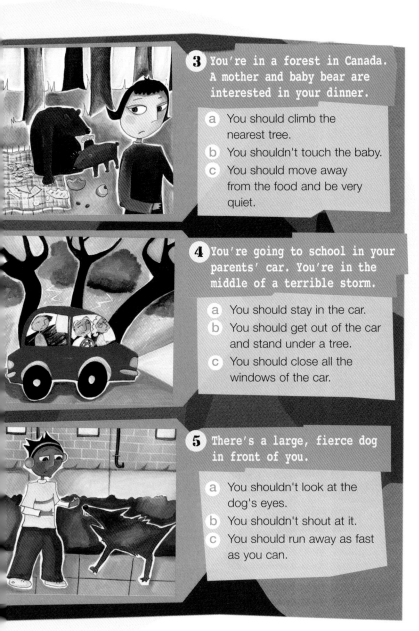

3 You're in a forest in Canada. A mother and baby bear are interested in your dinner.

a You should climb the nearest tree.

b You shouldn't touch the baby.

c You should move away from the food and be very quiet.

4 You're going to school in your parents' car. You're in the middle of a terrible storm.

a You should stay in the car.

b You should get out of the car and stand under a tree.

c You should close all the windows of the car.

5 There's a large, fierce dog in front of you.

a You shouldn't look at the dog's eyes.

b You shouldn't shout at it.

c You should run away as fast as you can.

4 Practice

a Write sentences with *should* or *shouldn't*. Make sure they're all good advice.

1 You should look carefully before you walk across the road.

1 You / look carefully before you walk across the road.

2 Everyone / eat lots of fruit and vegetables.

3 He / be so pessimistic. He / be more positive.

4 She / eat all that fast food. It isn't healthy.

5 They / get married now. They're too young.

6 You / smoke. It's very bad for you.

b Test a friend Write another sentence for 4a. Can your friend complete the sentence?

You / speak English in our English lessons.

You should speak English in our English lessons.

5 Key pronunciation /ʊ/ and /uː/

Listen and repeat the words.

1 /ʊ/ should could good put
2 /uː/ shoe food blue two

Listen and say these words. Are they the same or different? *1 different*

1 would true   2 look foot   3 soup book
4 juice move   5 boot cook   6 you good

6 Listening and speaking
'Talk to Tilda'

a Listen to the conversation on the radio between Tilda and Lisa. What's Lisa's problem?

b Listen again. Who says these things? Tilda or Lisa?

1 They were using my computer.

2 I was so angry.

3 They shouldn't use your computer.

4 They should ask you first.

5 I couldn't believe it.

6 I agree. I don't think they should read your emails.

7 They shouldn't read my emails.

8 You should talk to them more often.

9 You should be honest with them.

c What about you? Do you agree with Tilda? Share your ideas.

I think Lisa should ...

7 Writing and speaking *Advice*

Use what you know

Write a short letter asking for advice.

Dear Tilda,
I've got a problem. I'm always tired and I haven't got much energy. What's your advice?
Elvira.

Then work with a friend. Read your friend's letter and give some advice.

I think you should get more exercise.

In Step 3 you study
- *should*: questions

so that you can
- ask and answer questions with *should*
- share your opinions

My book review

Lord of the Flies   Ben Long

Lord of the Flies, by William Golding, is about a group of schoolboys. Their plane crashes and, for several months, they live on an island. There are no adults, so the boys must decide what to do on their own. They have a meeting and choose a leader. The story shows the different sides of human nature – good and bad. It's sometimes quite scary. I think it's a brilliant book. You should read it.

1 Reading   *Ben's review*

a Read Ben's book review. Is it positive or negative?

b Read the text again and answer the questions.

1   Where does the story take place?
2   Are there any adults on the island?
3   Do you think everything goes well?

2 Presentation   *What should we do?*

a 🎧 Look at the scene from *Lord of the Flies* and listen to the questions. What's happening?

a   It's the boys' first meal.
b   It's their first meeting.

b Match these answers with the questions.

1   Over there, under the trees.
2   Yes, they should. Everyone should do something.
3   No, we shouldn't. I don't want to share my things.

🎧 Listen and check.

a Should we have a leader?
b Who should it be?
c Should we build a house?
d Where should we build it?
e Should everyone share the work?
f Should we share our possessions?
g Should everyone vote?

3 Key grammar   *Questions with* should

Complete the answers.

Should	we have a leader? everyone vote?
Yes, we/they _____ . No, we/they _____ .	

G→ 13b

4 Practice

a Put the words in the right order and make questions.

1   *Should we share the cooking?*
1   we / cooking ? / share / should / the
2   be / should / leader ? / who / the
3   should / we / live ? / where
4   do ? / we / what / should
5   everyone / when / meet ? / should

b **Role play** If you have time, imagine you're one of the boys. Ask and answer questions in 2a and 4a.

Should we have a leader?

Yes, I think we should.

No, we shouldn't.

5 Writing and speaking   *Life's big questions*

Use what you know

Think of a question that's important to you. Use *should*. Ask at least four people and compare their opinions.

Should teenagers help at home?

Swim!

The big day

The weeks passed. School finished and Emily spent more and more time swimming. Finally, Saturday August 15th arrived – the day of the Picton Lake Race.

'How are you feeling?' asked Jack, as they arrived at the lake in Jack's car.

'I've got butterflies in my stomach,' said Emily, 'and, well …'

'What's the matter?' asked Jack. 'You're ready. Now just swim!'

'It's not that,' said Emily. 'It's Dad. I really wish …'

'Now, come on,' said Jack. 'You just go and change. There's something I must do.'

Emily went to get ready in the changing rooms near the lake. Jack walked down to the water and took out his mobile phone.

After his phone call, Jack walked back to find Emily. As he got nearer, he saw Tina Dawson. He saw her, but she couldn't see him. Dawson picked up a red water bottle outside the changing rooms. It was Emily's water bottle!

She quickly put something into Emily's bottle, and then walked away. Jack waited for a moment, then he went to look at the bottle. He opened it. He couldn't smell anything, but he was sure that there was something wrong. He ran after Dawson.

'Hey!' he said.

Dawson smiled at him, but Jack wasn't smiling.

'You put something into Emily's water bottle. I saw you. I'm going to tell Emily, and then we're going to tell the police.'

'I don't know what you mean,' said Dawson. She turned and walked down to the lake.

Questions

1 How did Emily feel when she arrived at the lake?
2 Who do you think Jack telephoned?
3 What did Tina Dawson do?
4 What did Jack want to do?

Extra exercises

1 Choose the right words.

1 Someone got _____ the office last night and stole some computers.
   a up
   b into
   c out of

2 The dog was very nervous and it ran _____ when it saw us.
   a after
   b along
   c away

3 I tried to push the piano into a corner, but it didn't _____ .
   a change
   b follow
   c move

4 She _____ the hill and stood at the top.
   a climbed
   b ran
   c walked

5 You mustn't _____ that spider. It's dangerous.
   a check
   b touch
   c find

6 He got _____ the boat and ran across the beach.
   a out of
   b along
   c up

2 Complete the sentences with *can* or *can't*.

1 The washing machine is broken. We _____ use it at the moment.

2 Where's my mobile? I _____ remember where I put it.

3 You _____ get a lot of different magazines at the newsagent's.

4 I've got some beefburgers and sausages. We _____ have a barbecue.

5 Jane _____ go bowling this evening. She's studying for her exams.

3 A teacher is talking to her class about a school trip. Complete the text with *can, can't, must* or *mustn't*.

The art gallery is about 10 kilometres from the school. We [1]_____ walk there, but we [2]_____ get there by bus. I've got some questions for you to answer, so you [3]_____ bring a notebook and a pen. When we're inside the gallery, you [4]_____ look at the paintings, but you [5]_____ touch them. Also, please don't bring cameras because you [6]_____ take photos. There's a café at the gallery so we [7]_____ get some soup or a sandwich before we leave.

4 Match the problems (1–6) with the advice (a–f).

1 I've got an important exam tomorrow.
2 I don't know how to answer these science questions.
3 I often get headaches.
4 Harry's always late.
5 I'd like to have some money to spend.
6 My brother always tells me I'm stupid.

a You shouldn't spend hours in front of your computer.
b You should try to find a job.
c You shouldn't listen to him.
d You should go to bed early tonight.
e You should talk to your teacher.
f You shouldn't wait for him.

5 Complete the conversations.

1 Can we make a phone call from the station?
   a Yes, you do.
   b Yes, it does.
   c Yes, we can.

2 Should I send this email to David?
   a He'll be OK.
   b No, you shouldn't.
   c I don't agree.

3 What can we have to eat?
   a There's some fruit in the kitchen.
   b Do you like apple juice?
   c No, sorry, you can't.

4 Why shouldn't people smoke?
   a Yes, they should.
   b They should stop immediately.
   c Because it's unhealthy.

5 What's your advice?
   a I think you should tell your parents.
   b He's got a good idea.
   c I can't believe it.

6 How do you say these sentences in your language?

1 Are you all right?
2 It really hurts.
3 Can you remember the way?
4 I'll be as quick as I can.
5 Smoking is bad for you.
6 You mustn't get cold.

Extra reading

A letter from Canada

What do you know about Canada?
Do you know anyone in Canada?

> Bison's Leap Ranch,
> Okotoks,
> Alberta,
> Canada.
> June 17th
>
> Hi! I'm Keri and I live in a place called Okotoks in Alberta, Canada. We live on a farm. It's called Bison's Leap Ranch, and it's enormous. We grow wheat here. We've got three hundred cows, about a hundred sheep, lots of hens, three dogs, two cats and five horses.
>
> The busiest time on our farm is September – that's harvest time. We don't see my dad for weeks – except when he runs into the kitchen for some food, and then runs out again!
>
> Our summers are short, but really hot. The autumn (we call it the fall) is beautiful. The sky is blue and the trees are red and gold. In the winter, we have snow for five or six months. We do lots of winter sports – skiing, ice hockey, skating and tobogganing.
>
> Canada is the second biggest country in the world. My Uncle Ed and Aunt Sandra live in Vancouver on the west coast and their daughter (my cousin) Sally lives in New Brunswick on the east coast. When they visit her, they drive for seven days!
>
> Alberta is a cool place to live. You should come and visit us one day. From my bedroom window, you can see the Rockies.
>
> I'm going to ride over to my friend Natalie's place now. That's the ranch next to ours.
>
> I'll write again soon.
>
> Keri

ABOUT CANADA

The Inuits were the first inhabitants of Canada, and they still live in northern Canada. They have their own language, traditions and culture.

Task

Read the letter from Keri, then answer these questions.

1 Does Keri live in a town?
2 Why is her dad busy in September?
3 What's the Canadian word for 'autumn'?
4 What's the weather like in the winter?
5 What do Keri and her friends do in the winter?
6 Is it very far from Vancouver to New Brunswick?
7 Does Keri live near the mountains?
8 When she visits her friend Natalie, how does she travel?

12 Who cares?

In Step 1 you study
- the names of everyday materials
- revision: expressing opinions; *must, should*

so that you can
- talk about recycling and the environment

1 Reading and speaking *Look around you!*

a Read the text then close your books. How many words can you remember for things in the environment?

What is the environment? Look around you!

The environment is:

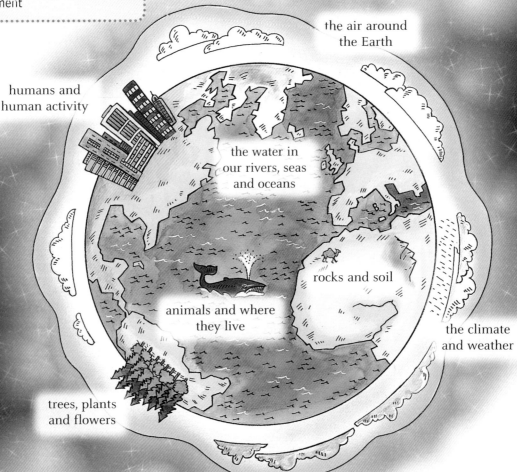

- the air around the Earth
- humans and human activity
- the water in our rivers, seas and oceans
- rocks and soil
- animals and where they live
- the climate and weather
- trees, plants and flowers

b **What about you?** Look at the survey and choose your answer. Then ask your friends:

A: What's your opinion?
B: I think it's worse. What do you think?
A: I really don't know!

Is our environment healthy or unhealthy? Is it getting better or worse? Here are the results of an Internet survey of teenagers.

Compared to 30 years ago, the global environment today is	
much worse	47%
worse	27%
a bit better	11%
I really don't know!	5%
about the same	4%
much better	3%

2 Key vocabulary *Everyday materials*

a 🕐 Read what Lisa says, then match the pictures with the <u>underlined</u> words. You've got three minutes!

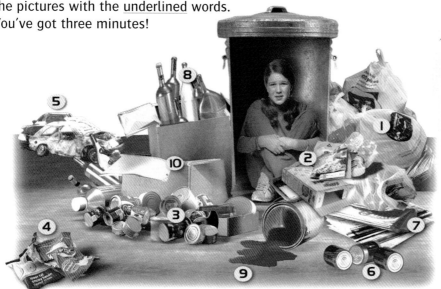

Would you like to live in a dustbin? Your answer is probably 'No, I wouldn't'. Well, look around you! Our world is full of rubbish: <u>cans</u>, <u>bottles</u>, <u>plastic bags</u>, <u>crisp packets</u>, <u>food cartons</u>, <u>newspapers and magazines</u>, <u>cardboard boxes</u>, <u>old cars</u> and all sorts of toxic things – <u>paint</u> and <u>old batteries</u>, for example. It's really disgusting!

🔊 Listen and check.

b **Test a friend** Look at the words in 2a and test a friend's spelling. Your friend mustn't look at the book!

> How do you spell 'plastic bag'?

Remember!

We can use *Would you like … ?*
with a noun:
Would you like some crisps?
or with a verb:
Would you like to live in the States?
Yes, I would. / No, I wouldn't.

3 Key pronunciation /æ/ *and* /e/

🔊 Listen and repeat the words.
1 /æ/ bag can plastic packet
2 /e/ bed said leg friend

🔊 Listen and say these words. Are they the same or different?

1 different

1 said sad	4 bread egg
2 head ten	5 black catch
3 man men	6 bad red

4 Speaking

a 🔊 Lisa and her friends are talking about the environment. Listen and follow in your book. Which things are true for you?

> I know we mustn't waste water, so I try to be careful.

> I sometimes recycle my magazines and I try to buy recycled paper.

> I know we should protect the environment, but I don't do very much.

> We walk a lot. We don't go everywhere in the car.

b **What about you?**
Say at least three things.

I don't use much water when I have a shower.
I reuse our plastic bags from the supermarket.
But I don't use recycled paper.

5 Speaking and writing *Green ideas*

Use what you know

How can we help the environment? Share your ideas and write them on the board.

We should recycle bottles and cans.
We mustn't go everywhere by car.

In Step 2 you study
● the first conditional

so that you can
● learn about our changing climate
● talk about results and consequences

1 Presentation *If he wins, he'll go to the Maldives*

a Do you know the answer to the question? Use your dictionaries and talk about the pictures and photos.

What's the connection between these beautiful islands in the Indian Ocean and the box of tissues in your bathroom?

b 🔊 Listen and read the conversation between Lisa and Ben. What's Lisa talking about?

a   an interesting competition
b   our changing climate
c   a holiday in Antarctica

Ben and Lisa are at the supermarket.
Ben's looking at a box of tissues.

BEN: Hey, there's a competition on the back of this box. 'Win a holiday in the Maldives.' I think I'll try it.

LISA: If you buy those, you won't go to the Maldives.

BEN: What do you mean?

LISA: Those tissues aren't made from recycled paper.

BEN: Lisa, what on earth are you talking about?

LISA: Paper comes from trees, right?

BEN: Right.

LISA: If we destroy trees, the climate will change. If the climate gets warmer, the ice caps will melt.

BEN: What are ice caps?

LISA: The ice in the Arctic and the Antarctic. Think about it! If the ice melts, where will it go?

BEN: Into the sea, I suppose.

LISA: Exactly. So the level of the sea will rise. And if that happens, the Maldives will disappear.

BEN: Disappear?

LISA: Yes. Under the sea! So if you buy those tissues, you'll never see the Maldives!

> **Try this!**
> Find the names of these islands.
>
> **IIAWAH ACROLLAM YLICIS**
> **DADINIRT AINIDRAS ACIAMAJ**

c Match the words in A with the words in B and make four sentences to go with the pictures.

A	B
1 If we destroy trees,	a the level of the sea will rise.
2 If the climate gets warmer,	b the climate will change.
3 If the ice caps melt,	c the Maldives will disappear.
4 If the level of the sea rises,	d the ice caps will melt.

2 Key grammar *First conditional*

Complete the examples, then complete the explanation.

> .... I win, I'll go to the Maldives.
> If we destroy trees, the climate .... change.
>
> *We use* If + ... , *and* will/won't + *verb when we talk about the future result of an action.*
>
> 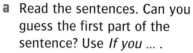 9a-b

3 Practice

Put the verbs in the right tense and write sentences.

1 If the climate gets too cold, life on Earth will die.

1 If the climate .... too cold, life on Earth .... (*get /die*)

2 If it .... too hot, the ice caps .... (*get /melt*)

3 If we .... our cars at home, the air .... cleaner. (*leave /be*)

4 If we .... them, tigers .... (*not protect / disappear*)

5 If the air .... polluted, we .... healthy. (*be / not be*)

6 If we .... anything, things .... better. (*not do / not get*)

4 Speaking and listening
Consequences

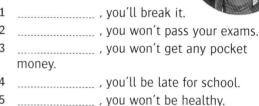

a Read the sentences. Can you guess the first part of the sentence? Use *If you ... .*

1 .... , you'll break it.
2 .... , you won't pass your exams.
3 .... , you won't get any pocket money.
4 .... , you'll be late for school.
5 .... , you won't be healthy.

b 🔊 Listen to Lisa and her parents. Were you right? Say the complete sentences.

5 Writing *Make a poster*

Use what you know

Use words from Steps 1 and 2 and make a poster with the title 'The Earth needs you'.

The Earth needs YOU! If we don't protect it, we'll lose it.

In Step 3 you
- read about the tiger
- listen to a song

1 Reading *Is it too late?*

a Read the article. Why are a lot of people worried about the tiger?

The Tiger

For many people, the tiger is the most beautiful and most exciting member of the cat family. But these fabulous creatures are in great danger. A hundred years ago, there were 100,000 tigers. They lived all over Asia. Today there are only 5,000.

In some countries, tigers mean 'money'. People use the tiger's body to make medicine. So the local people hunt the tiger and sell its body. And the forests where tigers live are disappearing, so they are losing their natural homes too.

Organisations like the World Wide Fund For Nature are trying to save the tiger, but it isn't easy. If we aren't careful, they will soon be extinct. And then the power and beauty of the wild tiger will only exist in our memories.

b Are these sentences true or false? Correct the false sentences.

1. The tiger is a member of the cat family.
2. A hundred years ago, there weren't many tigers.
3. People hunt and sell tigers.
4. Tigers are destroying their natural homes.
5. A lot of people want to help the tiger.
6. No one knows what will happen to the tiger.

2 Listening and speaking *Song*

a 🔊 Listen to the song and choose the best description.

a. It's a message to children all over the world.
b. It's a message from the tiger to all of us.
c. It's a message about animals in danger.

b 🔊 Listen again, then answer the questions. Share your ideas with the class.

1. What's happening in the first verse? Are there any problems?
2. What's happening in the second verse? Why is there 'danger in the air'?
3. Complete the tiger's message:
   It's a _____ world. But if you _____ , you _____ it for ever.

Swim!

The winner

'No Jack!' said Emily. 'Please don't tell the police! I want to swim against Tina Dawson. I want to beat her!'

'Well, OK,' said Jack. 'We must go, anyway. Come on. The race is starting in a minute.'

Emily looked at the crowd, but she couldn't see her dad.

Tina Dawson was standing just a few metres away, waiting for the start. Emily didn't look at her. She thought about Jack's voice, saying 'Just swim!'

The race started. Emily felt the cold water on her body. 'Swim!' she said to herself, again and again. 'Swim!'

After three hundred metres she was in front. The crowd cheered loudly. But now Dawson was in front. A minute passed, then Emily was the leader, but then it was Dawson again. The other side of Picton Lake wasn't far now. Ten metres from the finish, Dawson and Emily were together. Emily thought about her dad, her mum and Jack. Suddenly Dawson was behind her. The crowd cheered. Emily was the winner!

Tina Dawson walked away quickly. Emily walked up the beach, exhausted, but happy. She saw Jack running towards her. There was someone with him. It was her dad, and he was smiling!

'Emily!' he shouted, 'That was fantastic!' He kissed his daughter.

'But how ... ?'

'Jack asked me to come,' said her dad. 'I saw everything. I'm so proud of you and I know that your mother would be proud too.'

Then George Fieldman, the businessman, was there, shaking her hand. 'Excellent!' he said. 'The fastest time ever!'

Fieldman turned to Emily's dad. 'I would like to sponsor your daughter for the next two years,' he said. 'There'll be money, of course, for training.'

'And you can choose a trainer,' he said to Emily. 'I'm happy to pay for the best!'

Emily smiled a big smile and looked at Jack.

'I've already got the best,' she said.

Questions

1 Why didn't Emily want to go to the police?
2 What do you think helped her to win the race?
3 Did Emily's father watch the race?
4 What do you think Emily will do in the future?

Extra exercises

1 Match the words in A with the words in B.

A | B
1 a packet   a of paint
2 a carton   b of biscuits
3 a cardboard   c box
4 a can   d of fruit juice
5 a bottle   e bags
6 plastic   f of water

2 Choose the right words.

1 We _____ waste water.
   a shouldn't
   b can't
   c must

2 The air pollution is awful! It's getting _____ every year.
   a warmer
   b worse
   c dark

3 You can recycle those bottles. Don't put _____ in the dustbin.
   a it
   b him
   c them

4 Would you like _____ sailing?
   a go
   b to go
   c going

5 People should _____ their rubbish.
   a recycle
   b to recycle
   c will recycle

6 A: Would you like to sit down?
   B: _____
   a Yes, I would.
   b Yes, I like.
   c Yes, I do.

3 Which word is the odd one out?

1 lion   cheetah   tiger   elephant
2 river   sea   island   ocean
3 bird   flower   tree   plant
4 stone   rock   soil   climate
5 water   air   snow   ice
6 help   save   waste   protect
7 toxic   beautiful   brilliant   fabulous

4 Match the words in A with the words in B and make sentences.

A
1 If Sally catches the next train,
2 If you don't go to sleep now,
3 If they don't score another goal,
4 If you go out and talk to people,
5 If she doesn't train after school,
6 If they don't follow the map,

B
a they won't win the match.
b she won't get into the team.
c you'll wake up late tomorrow.
d they'll get lost.
e she'll arrive on time.
f you'll soon make friends.

5 Complete the sentences. Use the first conditional.

1 If we _destroy_ our forests, the Earth's climate _will change_ . (destroy/change)
2 If you _____ to the party, you _____ a great time. (come/have)
3 If she _____ me an email, I _____ it. (send/not answer)
4 If I _____ nervous, I _____ very well. (be/not sing)
5 If you _____ a coat, you _____ cold. (not wear/be)
6 If my brother _____ home soon, he _____ me with my homework. (get/help)
7 If Rosie _____ her project, the teacher _____ very angry. (not finish/be)

6 How do you say these sentences in your language?

1 What's your opinion?
2 It's really disgusting!
3 What on earth are you talking about?
4 Paper comes from trees, right? – Right.
5 The climate is already changing. – Exactly.
6 Is it getting better or worse?

Extra reading

The World Wide Fund For Nature

What does 'conservation' mean?

Do you know the names of any conservation groups in your country?

The **World Wide Fund For Nature** began in 1961. It is an international organisation, and it has 2,000 different conservation projects in different parts of the world. Its symbol is the famous giant panda.

The natural world is in great danger, and its most dangerous enemy is us – human beings. We are destroying the Earth's animals, plants and rainforests. The WWF is trying to protect them.

These are some of the problems.

- One in four animals (mammals, birds, reptiles and fish) are in danger.
- 13% of our plants and flowers are disappearing fast.
- 26 hectares of rainforest disappear *every minute*. Only 50% of the world's rainforest now remains.
- 60,000 whales and dolphins die every year in fishing nets.
- 50% of the world's coral reefs are in danger.

These are some of the WWF's successes.

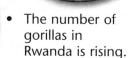

- In the 1960s there were only 100 rhinos* in Nepal. Now there are 600.

- The number of gorillas in Rwanda is rising.

- When the US government wanted to find oil in an important region of Alaska, the WWF stopped them.

You can help too.

For more information, go to the WWF website, or contact us at

Panda House, Weyside Park, Godalming, Surrey (UK).

* rhinoceros

A FINAL THOUGHT

'Think of all the beauty still left around you and be happy.'

Anne Frank

Task

Read the leaflet, then find this information.

1 Percentage of animals in danger.
2 Percentage of plants in danger.
3 Area of rainforest destroyed every minute.
4 Number of whales and dolphins killed every year.
5 Number of rhinos in Nepal 40 years ago.
6 Number of rhinos in Nepal now.

Module 6 Review

Language summary

1 can/must/should

Can, *must* and *should* have the same form for all persons (I, he, you, etc.). We use them with a verb in the infinitive form (without *to*).

> I can meet you after school.
> Danny can come too.
>
> You must wear your seat belt in the car.
> We must be careful.
>
> She should listen to your advice.
> They should go by train. It's quicker.

2 can

We use *can*, *can't* :

- to talk about abilities:
  Lee can play chess.
  I can't sing very well.
  Can you run fast? – Yes, I can. / No, I can't.

- to talk about what is and isn't possible:
  We can't use the microwave. It's broken.
  You can walk to the beach. It isn't far.

- to ask for permission, to give and refuse permission:
  Can we use your telephone, please? – Yes, of course you can.
  Can I have another biscuit? – No, sorry, you can't.
  You can go out tonight, but not on Sunday too.
  You can't wear that. It's mine!

Check that you can

2.1 ● understand and use *can*.

Match the sentences in A with the sentences in B. Then work with a friend and make eight conversations.

A
1 Can Lee play table tennis?
2 Sorry, but I can't come today.
3 Can we have two tickets for *The Last Samurai*?
4 Can I use your hairdryer?
5 You can't wear those!
6 Would you like to be in my team?
7 Where's Matt?
8 Can you hear that noise?

B
a Thanks, but I can't play basketball very well.
b Sure. I don't need it at the moment.
c I don't know. I can't see him.
d Yes, he's a brilliant player.
e Don't worry. I'll see you tomorrow.
f Yes, I can. There's something in that cupboard.
g Why not? They're my best trousers.
h That's nine fifty, please. It's Screen four.

2.2 ● ask for, give and refuse permission.

1 *Can we play snooker, please? — No, sorry, you can't.*
2 *Can I have some bacon? — Yes, of course you can.*

1 we / play snooker, please ? (*No*)
2 I / have some bacon ? (*Yes*)
3 we / take those cardboard boxes ? (*No*)
4 Sadie / use your sleeping bag ? (*No*)
5 I / share your book with you ? (*Yes*)
6 I / go abroad next year ? (*No*)
7 they / look around the hostel ? (*Yes*)
8 we / get into the boat now ? (*No*)

3 must

We use *must*, *mustn't* when we think that something is really important, or to talk about obligations or rules.

I/You/He/She We/They	must	hurry. go. stop now.
You	mustn't	take food into the library. smoke here.

Check that you can

● use *must* and *mustn't* + verb.

Complete these with *must* or *mustn't* + verb.

1. That's a poison arrow frog!
   We ___ it!

2. Are you OK?
   Yes, but I ___ a shower.

3. You ___ to school tomorrow.

4. We ___ to the top. The view will be fabulous.

4 *should*

We use *should/shouldn't* + verb

● when we think something is a good idea or a bad idea.

● when we ask for or give advice.

Affirmative and negative

I You He/She We	should	recycle newspapers. buy some glasses.
You They	shouldn't	drive so fast. eat a lot of sugar.

Questions and short answers

Should	I/you/he/she/ we/they	call the police?
Yes, No,	you/he/she/ we/they	should. shouldn't.
shouldn't = should not		

Check that you can

4.1 ● say if you think something is a good idea or not.

Complete the sentences with *should* or *shouldn't*.

1. It's really hot. You ___ sit in the sun.
2. Your essays are always brilliant. You ___ write a book.
3. That was stupid. You ___ think before you speak!
4. We ___ walk to work, but we're too lazy.
5. You ___ listen to other people's advice and you ___ interrupt all the time.
6. Don't put those bags in the dustbin. You ___ reuse them.
7. He ___ wear a jacket. He'll get cold.
8. Everyone ___ recycle their magazines and newspapers.

4.2 ● ask questions with *should*.

Put the words in the right order and make questions.

1. with / Natalie / go out / should / Matt ?
2. Lisa / more / be / should / honest ?
3. take ? / we / money / should / how much
4. say ? / what / I / should
5. we / should / boots ? / our / leave / where

5 The first conditional

We use the first conditional when we talk about possibilities in the future.

> *If* + present, *will/won't* + verb.
> If I **lose** my anorak again, my parents **will be** angry.
> If we**'re** lucky, we**'ll beat** them in the final.
> If he **doesn't take** a map, he**'ll get** lost.

Check that you can

● talk about possibilities in the future.

Complete the sentences, putting the verbs in the correct form.

1. *If we recycle our rubbish, we'll help the environment.*

1. If we ___ our rubbish, we ___ the environment. (*recycle/help*)
2. If it ___ nice tomorrow, I think I ___ to the beach. (*be/go*)
3. If you ___ any revision, you ___ your exams. (*not do/not pass*)
4. If they ___ the car, they ___ better. (*get out of/feel*)
5. If we ___ Tracey, she probably ___ to us again. (*not invite/not speak*)
6. If you ___ , they ___ you. (*run away/follow*)

Vocabulary

Games
chess
darts
snooker
table tennis

Verbs of action
(to) climb
(to) follow
(to) get into
(to) get out of
(to) move
(to) run after
(to) run away
(to) touch

The natural world
air
climate
flower
ocean
plant
river
rock
sea
soil
tree

Everyday materials
battery
bottle
box
can (*n.*)
cardboard
(food) carton
packet
paint (*n.*)
plastic

The environment
(to) destroy
(to) disappear
extinct
(to) get warmer
ice cap
in danger
level (of the sea)
(to) melt

polluted
(to) protect
(to) recycle
recycled
(to) reuse
(to) rise
rubbish
(to) save
(to) waste

Expressions
all sorts of things
Are you all right?
Be careful.
Exactly.
I really don't know.
I'll be as quick as
   I can.
Right?
What do you mean?
What on earth are
   you talking about?

Study skills 6   Studying at home

🕐 Think about good ways to work, and bad ways to work!
Match the things in the list with sentences 1 and 2. You've got four minutes! 1b, c, …

1 You'll probably work best if …
2 You won't do your best if …

a you're tired or hungry.
b you sit in a quiet place.
c you revise regularly.
d you do a bit of work nearly every day.
e you watch TV at the same time.
f you ask for help when you need it.
g you leave all your revision until the night before a test.
h you never do any homework.

Have you got any other ideas? Share your ideas with the class.

How's it going?

- ## Your rating

Look again at page 132–133. For each section give yourself a star rating:

Good ☆ ☆ ☆   Not bad ☆ ☆   I can't remember much ☆

- ## Vocabulary

Choose six words from the Vocabulary list and write them down.
Close your book and work with a friend. Ask:

> How do you spell … ?

- ## Test a friend

Look again at Units 11 and 12. Think of at least two questions, then ask a friend.

> What should you do if you meet a fierce dog?
> What does 'rubbish' mean?

- ## Correcting mistakes

Can you correct these mistakes?

1 ~~I must to go now~~.
2 ~~I don't can sing very well~~.
3 ~~If I will lose my book, my teacher is very angry~~.

- ## Your Workbook

Complete the Learning Diaries for Units 11 and 12.

Coursework 6 My window on the world

Read Matt's newsletter, then write about your country. Use pictures, photos and drawings.

A visit to my country

Hi! This is my last newsletter. I hope you enjoyed the others. This newsletter is an invitation to my country – and some advice.

You'll like my country! When are you coming?

My favourite place in the UK is the Lake District, in northwest England.

If you visit the UK, you'll need
- an umbrella, because it rains a lot.
- a dictionary, because the British aren't very good at foreign languages.
- a guide book, because there are some fabulous places to visit.

When you're in this country, you must remember
- to say 'Please' and 'Thank you'. The British are very polite!
- to stand in a queue. The British queue for everything.
- to talk about the weather. The British think it's really interesting.

Isn't it a lovely day!

Yes, it is. But it's going to rain this afternoon.

Visitors to the UK should
- try some fish and chips from a good fish and chip shop.
- go to the Eden Project in Cornwall.
- sit in Hyde Park in London and watch the world go by.

Eden Project

Grammar index

Communicative functions index

Unit 1
- Give facts *Penguins can't fly.*
- Ask for and give opinions *What do you think of ... ? I think it's great.*
- Agree and disagree *I agree with Jack. I don't agree.*
- Talk about things you like and don't like *I like football.*
- Ask for and give personal information *Where do you live?*

Unit 2
- Talk about your daily life *I walk to school with my sister.*
- Talk about what other people do *She wears a uniform.*
- Talk and ask about how often you do things *I never sing in the shower. How often do you tidy your room?*
- Describe different pastimes *We go swimming.*
- Talk about everyday routines *He reads before he goes to bed.*

Unit 3
- Say numbers in English *Three thousand nine hundred and seventy-eight.*
- Say the date in English *The second of October.*
- Talk about the past *She was born in 2002. Romeo loved Juliet.*
- Tell a story *He didn't go to school. He played in the streets.*

Unit 4
- Ask for information with *What ... ? Which ... ?* etc. *Where was Bob Marley born?*
- Ask and answer questions about the past *Did you meet all the stars?*
- Say when things happened in the past *Three months ago, she made her first record.*

Unit 5
- Describe a journey across a town *He went past the park ... .*
- Ask for and give directions *Can you tell me the way to the post office? Go along Queen Street and turn left.*
- Talk about things that are happening now *I'm waiting for my friends.*
- Talk about things that are generally true *Jono works as a disc jockey.*

Unit 6
- Describe a place in the past *There was a bridge across the river.*
- Talk about life in the past *The people were hunters.*
- Talk about actions in progress in the past *It was raining.*
- Talk about possibilities in the past *He could answer all the questions. He couldn't move his arm.*

Unit 7
- Describe and compare things *This car is bigger and more powerful than yours.*
- Talk about similarities and differences *Our house isn't as interesting as this.*
- Talk about people's possessions *Whose rucksack is this? It's Lisa's.*

Unit 8
- Compare one thing with the rest of a group *It's the longest river in the world.*
- Ask questions about places you know *What's the most popular café in ... ?*
- Talk about future plans and intentions *I'm going to get married next month.*
- Describe plans for a trip *We're going to travel by train.*
- Give your opinion *The best drink in our country is 'maté'.*

Unit 9
- Talk about things in the future *He'll be 75 years old. You won't like the food.*
- Ask and talk about important events in your life *Will I win the race tomorrow?*
- Make arrangements *Are you doing anything tonight?*

Unit 10
- Ask politely for food and drink *I'd like some rice. Could I have some soup?*
- Make polite offers *Would you like a drink?*
- Ask and answer questions about quantity *How much money will he have? How many emails will he write?*
- Talk about different lifestyles *We eat a lot of fast food.*

Unit 11
- Talk about what is and isn't possible *You can have mine. I can't hear anything.*
- Talk about rules and obligations *You must be careful. You mustn't talk.*
- Understand and give advice *You shouldn't smoke.*
- Talk about a problem and give your opinion *I think you should get more exercise. Everyone should vote.*

Unit 12
- Talk about the environment *I sometimes buy recycled paper.*
- Talk about results and consequences *If we destroy trees, the climate will change.*

Wordlist

Abbreviations *adj* = adjective   *Amer* = American English   *n* = noun   *prep* = preposition   *v* = verb
1.2 = Unit 1, Step 2   1.WF = Unit 1, Wild Flowers   8.S = Unit 8, Swim!   CW1 = Coursework, Module 1

A

a bit /ə bɪt/ 1.2
a couple of /ə ˈkʌpl əv/ 6.2
abroad /əˈbrɔːd/ 9.2
accent /ˈæksənt/ 1.WF
accident /ˈæksɪdənt/ 6.3
according to /əˈkɔːdɪŋ/ 2.WF
across /əˈkrɒs/ 3.1
activity /ækˈtɪvəti/ 12.1
addicted /əˈdɪktɪd/ 2.2
adventure /ədˈventʃə/ 7.2
adventurous /ədˈventʃərəs/ 5.1
advice /ədˈvaɪs/ 11.2
after that /ˈɑːftər ðæt/ 2.3
afterwards /ˈɑːftəwədz/ 8.S
against /əˈgentst/ 12.S
ago /əˈgəʊ/ 4.3
agree /əˈgriː/ 1.1
air /eər/ 6.2
airport /ˈeəpɔːt/ 5.3
alarm clock /əˈlɑːm klɒk/ 2.3
all over /ɔːl ˈəʊvə/ 12.3
all the time /ɔːl ðə taɪm/ 2.1
already /ɔːlˈredi/ 10.2
also /ˈɔːlsəʊ/ 1.3
angry /ˈæŋgri/ 11.2
(the) Antarctic /ænˈtɑːktɪk/ 2.1
anxious /ˈæŋkʃəs/ 2.2
any more /ˈeni mɔː/ 1.WF
anyway /ˈeniweɪ/ 9.3
appear /əˈpɪə/ 4.3
approximately
    /əˈprɒksɪmətli/ 10.2
argue /ˈɑːgjuː/ 2.2
around /əˈraʊnd/ 3.1
arrow /ˈærəʊ/ 8.1
as (=while) /æz/ 7.S
as usual /æz ˈjuːʒl/ 3.2
as well as /æz wel æz/ CW1
assassin /əˈsæsɪn/ CW2
assistant /əˈsɪstənt/ 4.2
astronomy /əˈstrɒnəmi/ 1.3
at least /ət liːst/ 7.2
athlete /ˈæθliːt/ 8.1
athletics /æθˈletɪks/ 1.3
attitude /ˈætɪtjuːd/ 9.1
author /ˈɔːθə/ CW2
available /əˈveɪləbl/ 11.1
average /ˈævərɪdʒ/ 2.3
(a few metres) away /əˈweɪ/ 12.S

B

babysit /ˈbeɪbɪsɪt/ 9.3
(on the) back (of) /bæk/ 12.2
backwards /ˈbækwədz/ 3.1
bacon /ˈbeɪkən/ 11.1
baked beans /beɪkt biːnz/ 10.1
baked potato
    /beɪkt pəˈteɪtəʊ/ 10.1
baker's /ˈbeɪkəz/ 6.1
ballad /ˈbæləd/ 3.3
bank /bæŋk/ 5.1
bar /bɑː/ 6.1
bargain /ˈbɑːgɪn/ 7.1
battery /ˈbætəri/ 12.1
beat (v) /biːt/ 2.2
beautiful /ˈbjuːtɪfl/ 1.1
beauty /ˈbjuːti/ 12.3
because of /bɪˈkɒz ɒv/ 1.WF
beefburger /ˈbiːfˌbɜːgə/ 10.1
before /bɪˈfɔː/ 2.3
belong (to) /bɪˈlɒŋ/ 3.3
best /best/ 8.3
better /ˈbetə/ 7.1
between /bɪˈtwiːn/ CW1
biscuit /ˈbɪskɪt/ 10.1
bite /baɪt/ 4.1
blink /blɪŋk/ 10.2
blood /blʌd/ 10.2
boat /bəʊt/ 3.2
boring /ˈbɔːrɪŋ/ 1.2
(at the) bottom (of) /ˈbɒtəm/ 6.2
bowl /bəʊl/ 3.WF
box /bɒks/ 12.1
brain /breɪn/ 10.2
bread /bred/ 10.1
break (v) /breɪk/ 6.3
bring /brɪŋ/ 9.2
broken /ˈbrəʊkən/ 6.3
build /bɪld/ 7.2
builder /ˈbɪldə/ 4.2
building /ˈbɪldɪŋ/ 6.1
burn /bɜːn/ 2.3
businessman /ˈbɪznɪsmæn/ 9.S
buy /baɪ/ 5.2
by (plane) /baɪ/ 2.1

C

cage /keɪdʒ/ 3.1.
camp (n) /kæmp/ 6.1
camp (v) /kæmp/ 8.2
campsite /ˈkæmpsaɪt/ 3.2
can (n) /kæn/ 12.1
canoeing /kəˈnuːɪŋ/ CW3

car park /kɑː pɑːk/ 5.1
caravan /ˈkærəvæn/ 3.2
cardboard /ˈkɑːdbɔːd/ 12.1
career /kəˈrɪə/ 4.2
(be) careful /ˈkeəfəl/ 12.1
carefully /ˈkeəfəli/ 11.2
Caribbean /ˌkærɪˈbiːən/ 11.2
carry /ˈkæri/ 5.2
carton /ˈkɑːtn/ 12.1
castle /ˈkɑːsl/ 6.1
century /ˈsentʃəri/ 4.1
change (your clothes)
    /tʃeɪndʒ/ 11.S
changing room /ˈtʃeɪndʒɪŋ
    ruːm/ CW3
(the) charts /ðə tʃɑːts/ 4.3
cheap /tʃiːp/ 7.1
check /tʃek/ 11.2
cheer (v) /tʃɪə/ 12.S
cheetah /ˈtʃiːtə/ 1.1
chemist's /ˈkemɪst/ 5.1
chess /tʃes/ 11.1
chocolate /ˈtʃɒklət/ 4.1
choose /tʃuːz/ 2.1
Christmas /ˈkrɪstməs/ CW5
civil rights /ˈsɪvl raɪts/ CW2
clean (v) /kliːn/ 6.3
clearly /ˈklɪəli/ 8.3
clever /ˈklevə/ 1.WF
climate /ˈklaɪmət/ 2.1
climb (v) /klaɪm/ 11.2
clothes shop /kləʊðz ʃɒp/ 5.1
club /klʌb/ 4.2
(sports) club /klʌb/ 5.3
coach (v) /kəʊtʃ/ 7.2
come down /kʌm daʊn/ 6.2
comfortable /ˈkʌmpftəbl/ 7.2
competitor /ˈkəmˈpetɪtə/ 8.S
computer animation
    /kəmˈpjuːtə ˌænɪˈmeɪʃn/ 4.2
connection /kəˈnekʃn/ 12.2
continue /ˈkənˈtɪnjuː/ 10.S
cookie (Amer) /ˈkʊki/ 10.2
cool /kuːl/ 5.2
(on the) corner /ˈkɔːnə/ 5.2
could /kʊd/ 6.3
Could I /kʊd aɪ/ 10.1
count /kaʊnt/ 6.WP
cow /kaʊ/ 4.2
crash (v) /kræʃ/ 11.3
crazy about
    /ˈkreɪzi əˈbaʊt/ 10.3
creature /ˈkriːtʃə/ 12.3
credit card /ˈkredɪt kɑːd/ 10.2

cross (v) /krɒs/ 11.2
crowd /kraʊd/ 12.S
cry (v) /kraɪ/ 6.2
cupboard /ˈkʌbəd/ 2.WF

D

dark (n) /dɑːk/ 1.1.
darts /dɑːts/ 11.1
dead /ded/ 3.3
department store
    /dɪˈpɑːtmənt stɔː/ 5.1
desert /ˈdezət/ 8.1
desert island /ˈdezət
    ˈaɪlənd/ 7.2
destroy /dɪˈstrɔɪ/ 12.2
die /daɪ/ 3.3.
digital camera /ˈdɪdʒɪtl
    ˈkæmərə/ 7.2
direct (a film) /dɪˈrekt/ 4.2
disappear /ˌdɪsəˈpɪə/ 11.2
disappointed
    /ˌdɪsəˈpɔɪntɪd/ 8.3
disc jockey /dɪsk ˈdʒɒki/ 4.2
dislike /dɪˈslaɪk/ 10.S
diving /ˈdaɪvɪŋ/ 2.1
down (there) /daʊn/ 11.1
drive /draɪv/ 3.2
drop /drɒp/ 6.2
dry /draɪ/ 7.2
duck /dʌk/ 7.2
dustbin /ˈdʌstbɪn/ 12.1
DVD player
    /ˌdiːviːˈdiː ˈpleɪə/ 7.2

E

early /ˈɜːli/ 8.S
(what on) earth … ? /ɜːθ/ 12.2
easily /ˈiːzəli/ 4.WF
Easter /ˈiːstə/ CW5
eclipse /ɪˈklɪps/ 8.3
ecology /iːˈkɒlədʒi/ 7.2
edition /ɪˈdɪʃn/ 9.1
electric toothbrush /ɪˈlektrɪk
    ˈtuːθbrʌʃ/ 7.2
(everyone) else /els/
end (n) /end/ 5.2
(in the) end /end/ 6.WF
enemy /ˈenəmi/ CW2
energy /ˈenədʒi/ 11.2
English Channel /ˈɪŋglɪʃ
    ˈtʃænl/ 3.1
enjoy /ɪnˈdʒɔɪ/ 1.3
entertainment
    /ˌentəˈteɪnmənt/ 4.1

environment
/ɪnˈvaɪərənmənt/ 12.1
equipment /ɪˈkwɪpmənt/ CW3
ethnic group
/ˈeθnɪk gruːp/ CW1
even /ˈiːvn/ 3.3
evening class
/ˈiːvnɪŋ klɑːs/ CW1
everything /ˈevriθɪŋ/ 6.3
everywhere /ˈevrihweə/ 12.1
Exactly. /ɪgˈzæktli/ 12.2
exam /ɪgˈzæm/ 6.3
excellent /ˈeksələnt/ 10.S
execute /ˈeksɪkjuːt/ 6.2
execution /ˌeksɪˈkjuːʃn/ 6.2
exhausted /ɪgˈzɔːstɪd/ 12.S
exhibition /ˌeksɪˈbɪʃn/ CW3
exist /ɪgˈzɪst/ 12.3
expensive /ɪkˈspentsɪv/ 7.1
experience /ɪkˈspɪəriənts/ 4.2
extinct /ɪkˈstɪŋkt/ 12.3

F

fabulous /ˈfæbjələs/ 12.3
factor /ˈfæktə/ 9.1
factory /ˈfæktəri/ 6.1
fail (an exam) /feɪl/ 9.2
fall /fɔːl/ 6.3
fall in love /fɔːl ɪn lʌv/ 9.2
far /fɑː/ 8.1
farmer /ˈfɑːmə/ 4.2
fascinating /ˈfæsɪneɪtɪŋ/ 2.1
fast /fɑːst/ 1.3
fast food /fɑːst fuːd/ 10.3
feel /fiːl/ 2.2
ferry /ˈferi/ 3.2
(a) few /fjuː/ 6.WF
fierce /fɪəs/ 11.2
film director
/fɪlm dɪˈrektə/ 4.1
film star /fɪlm stɑː/ 4.1
filming /ˈfɪlmɪŋ/ 4.2
finally /ˈfaɪnəli/ 10.S
find /faɪnd/ 7.3
find out /faɪnd aʊt/ 2.WF
finish (v) /ˈfɪnɪʃ/ CW1
fire /faɪə/ 6.3
fisherman /ˈfɪʃəmən/ 10.3
flag /flæg/ 8.2
flea /fliː/ 8.1
flower /ˈflaʊə/ 4.WF
fly (v) /flaɪ/ 8.2
follow /ˈfɒləʊ/ 11.2
for a long time
/fə ə lɒŋ taɪm/ 3.3
for long /fə lɒŋ/ 3.3
for once /fə wʌnts/ 6.WF
for sale /fə seɪl/ 7.1
former /ˈfɔːmə/ 8.S

fortune teller
/ˈfɔːtʃuːn ˈtelə/ 9.2
foundation /faʊnˈdeɪʃn/ CW2
free time /friː taɪm/ 2.1
fresh /freʃ/ 10.3
fridge /frɪdʒ/ 7.2
frog /frɒg/ 8.1
front door /frʌnt dɔː/ 5.WF
future /ˈfjuːtʃə/ 2.2

G

gardening /ˈgɑːdnɪŋ/ CW1
get (something) /get/ 7.3
get (the ferry) /get/ 3.2
get a job /get ə dʒɒb/ 9.2
get better /get ˈbetə/ 12.1
get cold /get kəʊld/ 11.1
get dark / get dɑːk/ 6.2
get dressed /get drest/ 2.3
get exercise
/get ˈeksəsaɪz/ 10.3
get home /get həʊm/ 2.3
get into /get ˈɪntə/ 11.2
get light /get laɪt/ 6.3
get lost /get lɒst/ 9.1
get married /get ˈmærɪd/ 9.2
get on (the bus) /get ɒn/ 9.S
get out /get aʊt/ 6.WF
get out of /get aʊt ɒv/ 11.2
get ready /get ˈredi/ 2.3
get undressed
/get ʌnˈdrest/ 2.3
get up /get ʌp/ 2.3
get worse /get wɜːs/ 12.1
giant /dʒaɪənt/ 1.2
glass /glɑːs/ 3.1
global /ˈgləʊbl/ 12.1
go across /gəʊ əˈkrɒs/ 5.1
go along /gəʊ əˈlɒŋ/ 5.1
go back /gəʊ bæk/ 11.1
go camping
/gəʊ ˈkæmpɪŋ/ CW5
go into /gəʊ ˈɪntə/ 3.WF
go on a boat trip /gəʊ ɒn ə
bəʊt trɪp/ 3.2
go out /gəʊ aʊt/ 1.3
go out with (someone) /gəʊ
aʊt wɪð/ 9.2
go past /gəʊ pɑːst/ 5.1
go shopping /gəʊ ˈʃɒpɪŋ/ 1.2
go to sleep /gəʊ tə sliːp/ 2.3
go tobogganing /gəʊ
təˈbɒgənɪŋ/ CW5
go wrong /gəʊ rɒŋ/ 9.1
Good luck! /gʊd lʌk/ 4.2
government
/ˈgʌvənmənt/ CW1
grapes /greɪps/ 10.1
ground /graʊnd/ 1.1

guard (n) /gɑːd/ 6.2
guide book /gaɪd bʊk/ CW6

H

hairdryer /ˈheədraɪər/ 7.2
hall /hɔːl/ 11.1
hard /hɑːd/ 3.3
hate /heɪt/ 1.3
have a barbecue /hæv ə
ˈbɑːbɪkjuː/ 10.1
have a drink /hæv ə
drɪŋk/ 2.3.
head (teacher) /hed/ 1.WF
headline /ˈhedlaɪn/ 9.S
healthy /ˈhelθi/ 10.3
helicopter /ˈhelɪkɒptə/ 11.1
help (n) /help/ 11.1
Help yourself! /help
jɔːˈself/ 10.1
hero /ˈhɪərəʊ/ 3.2
hide /haɪd/ 2.WF
high /haɪ/ 8.1
himself /hɪmˈself/ 7.2
hit (v) /hɪt/ 2.2
hole /həʊl/ 1.1.
hope /həʊp/ CW5
horrible /ˈhɒrəbl/ 5.WF
hospital /ˈhɒspɪtəl/ 5.1
hotel /həʊˈtel/ 3.2
How long ...? /haʊ lɒŋ/ 8.1
How much is ...? /haʊ
mʌtʃ ɪz/ 7.1
How often ...? /haʊ ˈɒfən/ 2.2
How tall ...? /haʊ tɔːl/ 8.1
human /ˈhjuːmən/ 12.1
human nature /ˈhjuːmən
ˈneɪtʃə/ 11.3
hunt (v) /hʌnt/ 12.3
hunter /ˈhʌntə/ 6.1
hurt /hɜːt/ 11.1

I

ice cap /aɪs kæp/ 12.2
ice hockey /aɪs ˈhɒki/ 10.3
ill /ɪl/ 1.WF
immediately /ɪˈmiːdiətli/ 11.2
in danger /ɪn ˈdeɪndʒə/ 11.2
in love /ɪn lʌv/ 3.3
incredible /ɪnˈkredɪbl/ 8.1
industry /ˈɪndəstri/ 4.2
interview /ˈɪntəvjuː/ 9.1
invent /ɪnˈvent/ 4.1
inventions /ɪnˈventʃnz/ 7.2
invitation /ˌɪnvɪˈteɪʃn/ CW6
island /ˈaɪlənd/ 7.2
its /ɪts/ 8.1

J

jet /dʒet/ 8.1
jogging /ˈdʒɒgɪŋ/ 2.2
joke /dʒəʊk/ 3.WF
journey /ˈdʒɜːni/ 3.1
judge /dʒʌdʒ/ 3.3
jump /dʒʌmp/ 8.1
just /dʒʌst/ CW1

K

key /kiː/ 9.1
keyboard /ˈkiːbɔːd/ 7.1
kill /kɪl/ 3.3
(a hundred) kilometres (an hour)
/kɪˈlɒmɪtəz/ 1.1
kindly /ˈkaɪndli/ 8.S
king /kɪŋ/ 4.1
kingdom /ˈkɪŋdəm/ 8.1
kiss /kɪs/ 12.S
knee /niː/ 1.1
know (someone) /nəʊ/ 5.2

L

landscape /ˈlændskeɪp/ 4.1
large /lɑːdʒ/ 1.1
laugh (n) /lɑːf/ 5.WF
laugh (v) /lɑːf/ 6.2
lawyer /ˈlɔɪə/ 7.S
(on the) left /left/ 5.1
length /leŋkθ/ 8.1
level /ˈlevl/ 12.2
library /ˈlaɪbrəri/ 2.WF
lifestyle /ˈlaɪfstaɪl/ 10.3
lifetime /ˈlaɪftaɪm/ 10.2
light (n) /laɪt/ 6.2
light (adj) /laɪt/ 6.3
like (prep) /laɪk/ 9.2
litre /ˈliːtə/ 10.2
local /ˈləʊkl/ 1.3
lock (v) /lɒk/ 5.WF
lock (n) /lɒk/ 6.WF
look (unhappy) /lʊk/ 3.WF
look around /lʊk əˈraʊnd/ 4.WF
look for /lʊk fɔː/ 4.WF
lord /lɔːd/ 4.1
lose /luːz/ 12.3
lots of /lɒts əv/ 4.2
loud /laʊd/ 4.WF
loudly /ˈlaʊdli/ 5.WF
lounge /laʊndʒ/ CW3

M

machine /məˈʃiːn/ 7.2
made from /meɪd frɒm/ 12.2
magic /ˈmædʒɪk/ 4.1
main /meɪn/ 1.3
make a phone call /meɪk ə
fəʊn kɔːl/ 10.2
make a record /meɪk ə

/ˈrekɔːd/ 4.3
make friends
/meɪk frendz/ 9.1
(The) Maldives
/ðə ˈmɔːldiːvz/ 12.2
manager /ˈmænɪdʒə/ 4.1
maybe /ˈmeɪbi/ 4.WF
mechanic /mɪˈkænɪk/ 4.2
media production /ˈmiːdiə
prəˈdʌkʃn/ 4.2
medicine /ˈmedsn/ 12.3
medieval /ˌmediˈiːvl/ 6.1
meet (friends) /miːt/ 1.3
meeting /ˈmiːtɪŋ/ 11.3
melt /melt/ 12.2
memory /ˈmeməri/ 12.3
mess (n) /mes/ 2.3
mew /mjuː/ 5.WF
microscope
/ˈmaɪkrəskəʊp/ 6.WF
microwave /ˈmaɪkrəʊweɪv/ 7.2
(in the) middle (of) /ˈmɪdl/ 10.3
millionaire /ˌmɪljəˈneə/ 10.2
millions (of) /ˈmɪljənz/ 4.3
mistake /mɪˈsteɪk/ 9.1
mixture /ˈmɪkstʃə/ CW1
model /ˈmɒdl/ CW3
modern /ˈmɒdn/ 6.2
more than /mɔː ðən/ 7.2
motivate /ˈməʊtɪveɪt/ CW2
mouse /maʊs/ 7.1
move /muːv/ 3.2

N

natural /ˈnætʃrəl/ 12.3
nearly /ˈnɪəli/ 2.2
necessary /ˈnesəsəri/ 1.1
negative /ˈnegətɪv/ 9.1
newsagent's
/ˈnjuːzˌeɪdʒənts/ 5.1
newspaper /ˈnjuːsˌpeɪpə/ 1.3
next /nekst/ 2.2
no one /ˈnəʊwʌn/ 2.WF
note /nəʊt/ 11.1
notes /nəʊts/ 4.WF
nothing /ˈnʌθɪŋ/ 3.WF
notice (v) /ˈnəʊtɪs/ 9.S

O

offer /ˈɒfə/ 9.S
on fire /ɒn faɪə/ 6.3
on his own /ɒn hɪz əʊn/ 3.1
once /wʌns/ 2.2
opinion /əˈpɪnjən/ 1.2
optimistic /ˌɒptɪˈmɪstɪk/ 9.1
organisation
/ˌɔːgənaɪˈzeɪʃn/ 12.3
outside /ˌaʊtˈsaɪd/ 2.1
owl /aʊl/ 1.1
owner /ˈəʊnə/ 5.1

P

packet /ˈpækɪt/ 12.1
paint (n) /peɪnt/ 12.1
pale /peɪl/ 6.2
paradise /ˈpærədaɪs/ 7.2
part /pɑːt/ 1.1
pass (time) /pɑːs/ 6.WF
pass an exam /pɑːs ən
ɪgˈzæm/ 9.2
pastime /ˈpɑːstaɪm/ 2.2
pay for /peɪ fɔː/ 12.S
peas /piːz/ 10.1
perhaps /pəˈhæps/ 2.2
pessimistic /ˌpesɪˈmɪstɪk/ 9.1
pick up /ˈpɪk ʌp/ 11.S
picnic /ˈpɪknɪk/ CW5
piece (of advice) /piːs/ 11.2
plane /pleɪn/ 2.1
planet /ˈplænɪt/ 4.1
plant (n) /plɑːnt/ 12.1
plastic /ˈplæstɪk/ 7.2
platform /ˈplætfɔːm/ 5.2
play a tape /pleɪ ə teɪp/ 6.WF
play cards /pleɪ kɑːdz/ 2.1
playing field
/ˈpleɪɪŋ ˈfiːld/ 4.WF
poison (n) /ˈpɔɪzn/ 8.1
police /pəˈliːs/ 5.1
police station
/pəˈliːs ˈsteɪʃn/ 5.1
polite /pəˈlaɪt/ CW6
polluted /pəˈluːtɪd/ 7.2
population /ˌpɒpjəˈleɪʃn/ CW1
porridge /ˈpɒrɪdʒ/ 11.1
positive /ˈpɒzətɪv/ 9.1
post office /pəʊst ˈɒfɪs/ 5.1
potato /pəˈteɪtəʊ/ 10.1
power /paʊə/ 7.2
powerful /ˈpaʊəfl/ 1.1
prime minister /praɪm
ˈmɪnɪstə/ CW1
printer /ˈprɪntə/ 7.1
prison /ˈprɪzn/ 3.3
probably /ˈprɒbəbli/ 9.1
professional /prəˈfeʃənl/ 8.S
project /ˈprɒdʒekt/ 1.2
proof /pruːf/ 5.WF
protect /prəˈtekt/ 12.1
proud /praʊd/ 12.S
psychologist
/saɪˈkɒlədʒɪst/ 9.1
pudding /ˈpʊdɪŋ/ CW5
push /pʊʃ/ 3.2
put /pʊt/ 3.2

Q

queen /kwiːn/ 3.1
queue (n) /kjuː/ 10.1
quick /kwɪk/ 6.3

quickly /ˈkwɪkli/ 6.S
quiet /ˈkwaɪət/ 6.1
quietly /ˈkwaɪətli/ 9.S
quite /kwaɪt/ 3.2
quite a lot /kwaɪt ə lɒt/ 10.2

R

race (n) /reɪs/ 8.S
racing car /ˈreɪsɪŋ kɑː/ 4.2
radioactive
/ˌreɪdiəʊˈæktɪv/ 4.1
rare /reə/ 4.WF
rating /ˈreɪtɪŋ/ 8.3
recent /ˈriːsnt/ 2.2
(a world) record /ˈrekɔːd/ 3.1
record (n) /ˈrekɔːd/ 3.1
record (v) /rɪˈkɔːd/ 4.3
recycle /ˌriːˈsaɪkl/ 12.1
recycled /ˌriːˈsaɪkld/ 12.1
relatives /ˈrelətɪvz/ 8.2
reply /rɪˈplaɪ/ 5.WF
research /rɪˈsɜːtʃ/ 2.1
reuse /ˌriːˈjuːz/ 12.1
rice /raɪs/ 10.1
ride (n) /raɪd/ CW5
(on the) right /raɪt/ 5.1
ring /rɪŋ/ 4.1
rise /raɪz/ 12.2
roast /rəʊst/ CW5
rock /rɒk/ 12.1
roller coaster
/ˈrəʊlə ˈkəʊstə/ 8.2
roller-blading
/ˈrəʊlə ˈbleɪdɪŋ/ 2.2
Roman /ˈrəʊmən/ 6.1
round /raʊnd/ 6.1
rubbish /ˈrʌbɪʃ/ 12.1
rucksack /ˈrʌksæk/ 3.2
rule /ruːl/ 11.1
run /rʌn/ 11.2
run after /rʌn ˈɑːftə/ 11.2
run away /rʌn əˈweɪ/ 11.2
run back /rʌn bæk/ 2.WF
run down /rʌn daʊn/ 6.WF

S

sail (v) /seɪl/ 3.1
sauce /sɔːs/ 10.1
save /seɪv/ 12.3
scary /ˈskeəri/ 11.3
schoolboys /ˈskuːlbɔɪz/ 11.3
scorpion /ˈskɔːpiən/ 3.1
screen /skriːn/ 7.1
second (n) /ˈsekənd/ 1.3
secretary /ˈsekrətri/ 4.2
section /ˈsekʃn/ 4.2
seem /siːm/ 10.3
sell /sel/ 4.1
serve /sɜːv/ 4.2
session /ˈseʃn/ 9.S

several /ˈsevrəl/ 5.1
shake (hands) /ʃeɪk/ 6.WF
share /ʃeə/ 7.2
sheriff /ˈʃerɪf/ 3.3
ship /ʃɪp/ 2.1
shock /ʃɒk/ 5.1
shoe shop /ʃuː ʃɒp/ 5.1
shoot /ʃuːt/ 3.3
shop assistant
/ʃɒp əˈsɪstənt/ 4.2
short /ʃɔːt/ 7.1
show /ʃəʊ/ 11.3
sign language /saɪn
ˈlæŋgwɪdʒ/ 1.1
silly /ˈsɪli/ 1.2
simple /ˈsɪmpl/ 6.1
size /saɪz/ 8.1
skyscraper /ˈskaɪˌskreɪpə/ 6.1
sleep (n) /sliːp/ 10.2
sleeping bag /ˈsliːpɪŋ bæg/ 3.2
slow /sləʊ/ 7.1
slowly /ˈsləʊli/ 6.WF
smell (v) /smel/ 11.S
smile /smaɪl/ 1.WF
smoke (v) /sməʊk/ 11.1
smoke (n) /sməʊk/ 6.3
snooker /ˈsnuːkə/ 11.1
soil /sɔɪl/ 12.1
solar power /ˈsəʊlə paʊə/ 7.2
solar system
/ˈsəʊlə ˈsɪstəm/ 8.1
soup /suːp/ 10.1
space /speɪs/ CW3
space station
/speɪs ˈsteɪʃn/ 8.3
spacesuit /speɪsˈt/ CW3
speaker /ˈspiːkə/ 7.1
special /ˈspeʃl/ 3.1
speed /spiːd/ 3.1
spend (time) /spend/ 2.2
sponsor (v) /spɒnsə/ 12.S
square /skweə/ 5.1
stand up /stænd ʌp/ 7.S
star /stɑː/ 2.1
stay /steɪ/ 3.1
steal /stiːl/ 3.3
steps /steps/ 6.2
stereo /ˈsteriəʊ/ 7.2
still /stɪl/ 4.2
Stone Age /stəʊn eɪdʒ/ 6.1
stop (= prevent) /stɒp/ 6.WF
storm /stɔːm/ 11.2
strange /streɪndʒ/ 1.2
study (n) /ˈstʌdi/ 8.3
study (v) /ˈstʌdi/ 4.1
stupid /ˈstjuːpɪd/ 4.1
subject /ˈsʌbdʒɪkt/ 1.2
succeed /səkˈsiːd/ CW2
suddenly /ˈsʌdnli/ 3.2
sun /sʌn/ 8.3

suppose /sə'pəʊz/ 1.2
survey /'sɜːveɪ/ 2.1
survivor /sə'vaɪvə/ 11.2
swimsuit /'swɪmsuːt/ 9.S

T

table tennis /'teɪbl 'tenɪs/ 11.1
take /teɪk/ 3.2
take an exam /teɪk æn ɪg'zæm/ 9.2
take out /teɪk aʊt/ 11.S
take place /teɪk pleɪs/ 4.1
tall /tɔːl/ 7.1
tape recorder /teɪp rɪ'kɔːdə/ 5.WF
taxi driver /'tæksi 'draɪvə/ 4.2
team /tiːm/ 9.1
telescope /'telɪskəʊp/ 8.3
tell /tel/ CW1
temperature /'temprətʃə/ CW4
tent /tent/ 3.2
term /tɜːm/ 9.1
terrible /'terəbl/ 2.WF
text (v) /tekst/ 3.WF
theme park /θiːm pɑːk/ 8.2
think about /θɪŋk ə'baʊt/ 5.3
through /θruː/ 6.2
throw /θrəʊ/ 6.WF

tidy (v) /'taɪdi/ 2.2
times (a week) /taɪmz/ 2.2
together /tə'geðə/ 3.3
tons /tʌnz/ 10.2
too much /tuː mʌtʃ/ CW5
(at the) top (of) /tɒp/ 6.2
top score /tɒp skɔːr/ 2.2
touch /tʌtʃ/ 11.2
towards /tə'wɔːdz/ 9.1
tower /taʊər/ 6.2
town hall /taʊn hɔːl/ 6.1
toxic /'tɒksɪk/ 12.1
trainer /'treɪnə/ 7.S
travel (v) /'trævl/ 8.3
travel (n) /'trævl/ 2.1
tree /triː/ 1.1
trip /trɪp/ 3.2
(be in) trouble /bi: ɪn 'trʌbl/ 6.WF
(the) tube /ðə tjuːb/ 5.3
turkey /'tɜːki/ CW5
turn (left/right) /tɜːn/ 5.1
TV studio /ˌtiː'viː 'stjuːdiəʊ/ 3.1
twice (a year) /twaɪs/ 2.1

U

umbrella /ʌm'brelə/ CW6
underground railway /'ʌndəgraʊnd 'reɪlweɪ/ 5.3
unhappy /ʌn'hæpi/ 3.WF
unhealthy /ʌn'helθi/ 10.3
unlock /ʌn'lɒk/ 6.WF
unlucky /ʌn'lʌki/ 9.1

V

veggieburger /'vedʒi,bɜːgə/ 10.1
vegetables /'vedʒtəblz/ 10.3
village /'vɪlɪdʒ/ 6.1
visitor /'vɪzɪtə/ 6.2
voice /vɔɪs/ 3.3
vote (v) /vəʊt/ 11.3

W

wait for /weɪt fɔːr/ 5.2
waitress /'weɪtrəs/ 4.2
wake up /weɪk ʌp/ 2.3
walk away /wɔːk ə'weɪ/ 11.S
walk back /wɔːk bæk/ 2.WF
walk through /wɔːk θruː/ 6.2
walk up /wɔːk ʌp/ 12.S
walk up to /wɔːk ʌp tuː/ 5.WF
wallaby /'wɒləbi/ 9.2

warm /wɔːm/ 9.2
washing machine /'wɒʃɪŋ mə'ʃiːn/ 7.2
waste (v) /weɪst/ 12.1
way of life /weɪ ɒv laɪf/ 7.2
weigh /weɪ/ 10.2
Welcome to ... ! /'welkəm/ 5.2
wet /wet/ CW4
while /'waɪl/ 5.2
whole /həʊl/ 3.WF
whose /huːz/ 7.3
wild /waɪld/ 4.WF
win /wɪn/ 9.1
wind /wɪnd/ 3.3
wings /wɪŋz/ 1.1
winner /wɪnə/ 9.S
wish (v) /wɪʃ/ 11.S
without /wɪ'ðaʊt/ 4.WF
work (n) /wɜːk/ 2.1
work (v) (machine) /wɜːk/ 6.WF
worried /'wʌrid/ 12.3
worry /'wʌri/ 2.2
worse /wɜːs/ 8.3
worst /wɜːst/ 8.3

Y

youth hostel /juːθ 'hɒstəl/ 11.1

Irregular verbs

Verb	Past simple	Verb	Past simple	Verb	Past simple
be	was/were	find	found	see	saw
beat	beat	fly	flew	sell	sold
become	became	forget	forgot	send	sent
begin	began	get	got	sing	sang
bite	bit	give	gave	sit	sat
break	broke	go	went	sleep	slept
bring	brought	grow	grew	speak	spoke
build	built	have	had	spend	spent
buy	bought	hear	heard	stand	stood
can/be able to	could	know	knew	steal	stole
catch	caught	leave	left	swim	swam
choose	chose	lose	lost	take	took
come	came	make	made	teach	taught
cost	cost	meet	met	tell	told
do	did	pay	paid	think	thought
drink	drank	put	put	understand	understood
drive	drove	read	read	wake	woke
eat	ate	ride	rode	wear	wore
fall	fell	ring	rang	win	won
feel	felt	run	ran	write	wrote
fight	fought	say	said		

Spelling notes

1 Word + -s

Look at what happens when we add -s to:

- words which end in **-s, -sh, -ch, -x**:

  a bus ➤ two bus**es**
  I cross ➤ he cross**es**
  I wash ➤ he wash**es**
  I catch ➤ he catch**es**
  a box ➤ two box**es**

- words which end in **-o** often add **-es**:

  a potato ➤ two potato**es**
  I do ➤ he do**es**

  BUT a radio ➤ two radio**s**
  a stereo ➤ two stereo**s**
  a photo ➤ two photo**s**

- words which end in **consonant + -y**:

  a family ➤ two famil**ies**
  they fly ➤ he fl**ies**

  BUT words which end in **vowel + -y**:
  I say ➤ he sa**ys**
  a day ➤ two da**ys**

- words which end in **-f/-fe**:

  a shelf ➤ two shel**ves**
  a life ➤ two li**ves**

2 Irregular plurals

Some nouns have an 'irregular' plural form.

a child ➤ two children
a person ➤ two people
a man ➤ two men
a woman ➤ two women

a foot ➤ two feet
a tooth ➤ two teeth

3 Word + -ing

Look at what happens when we add -ing to these verbs:

take ➤ tak**ing**
have ➤ hav**ing**
run ➤ run**ning**
get ➤ get**ting**
swim ➤ swim**ming**
travel ➤ travel**ling**

4 Past simple + -ed

Look at the spelling of these verbs in the past simple:

live ➤ live**d**
move ➤ move**d**
drop ➤ drop**ped**
travel ➤ travel**led**
carry ➤ carr**ied**
tidy ➤ tid**ied**

5 Comparatives

Adjectives with one syllable, add -er or -r:

cold ➤ cold**er**
tall ➤ tall**er**
nice ➤ nice**r**
large ➤ large**r**

BUT big ➤ big**ger**
hot ➤ hot**ter**

For adjectives which end in consonant + -y:

pretty ➤ prett**ier**
happy ➤ happ**ier**

6 Superlatives

Adjectives with one syllable, add -est or -st:

cold ➤ cold**est**
long ➤ long**est**
nice ➤ nice**st**
large ➤ large**st**

BUT big ➤ big**gest**
hot ➤ hot**test**

For adjectives which end in consonant + -y:

pretty ➤ prett**iest**
happy ➤ happ**iest**

Phonetic symbols

Consonants

/p/	**p**en	/s/	**s**ee	/ʒ/	u**s**ually
/b/	**b**e	/z/	trou**s**ers	/dʒ/	**g**enerally
/t/	**t**oo	/w/	**w**e		
/d/	**d**o	/l/	**l**isten		
/k/	**c**an	/r/	**r**ight		
/g/	**g**ood	/j/	**y**ou		
/f/	**f**ive	/h/	**h**e		
/v/	**v**ery	/θ/	**th**ing		
/m/	**m**ake	/ð/	**th**is		
/n/	**n**ice	/ʃ/	**sh**e		
/ŋ/	si**ng**	/tʃ/	**ch**eese		

Vowels

/æ/	m**a**n
/ɑː/	f**a**ther
/e/	t**e**n
/ɜː/	th**ir**teen
/ə/	m**o**ther
/ɪ/	s**i**t
/iː/	s**ee**
/ʊ/	b**oo**k
/uː/	f**oo**d
/ʌ/	**u**p
/ɒ/	h**o**t
/ɔː/	f**our**

Diphthongs

/eɪ/	gr**ea**t
/aɪ/	f**i**ne
/ɔɪ/	b**oy**
/ɪə/	h**ear**
/eə/	ch**air**
/aʊ/	t**ow**n
/əʊ/	g**o**
/ʊə/	p**ure**

Songs

Unit 2 Monday Morning

The alarm clock rings
But I can't wake up.
Another week begins.
I don't want to get up.

Chorus

A: Where's my shirt? **B:** Your toast is burning!
A: Where's my lunch? **B:** Don't forget your bus pass!
A: Where's my bag? **B:** Your hair's a mess!
A: I hate ... **B:** I hate ...
A&B: We hate Monday!

The alarm clock rings,
It's ten to eight.
Another week begins.
I'm always tired and always late.

(Chorus x2)

Unit 4 Last Night

It was a year ago,
You decided to leave.
You didn't even say goodbye.
You closed the door.
I heard the sound of your car.
But did you hear me cry?

Chorus
And then last night the telephone rang.
It was your voice at the end of the line.
But you can't just come back into my world
And then think everything's fine again.

It was a year ago
You walked out of my life.
You didn't even tell me why.
So I closed my heart.
I threw the photos away.
I said I didn't mind.

(Chorus)

Unit 5 Smiling

Hey! Hey! I'm not smiling. Hey! Hey! I'm not smiling.
I'm waiting for my friends.
I'm sitting on the wall.
I'm listening to hip-hop.
I'm not smiling. I'm bored.
Just watching all the people while they're walking
and they're talking.

Hey! Hey! I'm not smiling. Hey! Hey! I'm not smiling.
She's standing on the corner.
I don't think that I know her.
She's drinking cool cola.
Is she waiting for someone?
Hey! She's looking at me.
Hey! She's smiling at me.
Hey! I'm smiling now. I'm smiling now.
I'm smiling now. I'm smiling now.

I'm waiting for my friends.
I'm sitting on the wall.
I'm smiling now. I'm smiling now.

Unit 9 Sweet Dreams

Sweet dreams, sweet dreams. (x2)

The old man is sitting on a bench in the park.
The day is disappearing and the sky is getting dark.
Where will he sleep tonight?
Will he be warm tonight?
What will tomorrow bring?

Sweet dreams, sweet dreams.

The people are leaving, they turn their eyes away.
No one ever talks to him, they don't know what to say.
Where will they sleep tonight?
Will they be warm tonight?
What will tomorrow bring?

Unit 12 Song of the Tiger

It's a beautiful day today.
The sun is shining,
The air is cool.
I can see my children playing by the river.
It's a bright new morning
And the trees are touching the sky.

Chorus
It's a wonderful world
But if you don't change,
You'll lose it for ever.
So listen to the song of the tiger.

There are noises in the forest now.
There's danger in the air.
I can see the men coming with their machines.
But they can't see me.
They don't care about the tiger.

(Chorus)
It's a wonderful world.
It's in your hands.
You'll lose it for ever,
If you don't listen to the song of the tiger.
Listen to the song of the tiger.

Theory of Music Grade 2
November 2018

T
CC

CW00405186

Your full name (as on appointment form). Please use BLOCK CAPITALS.

_____

Your signature   Registration number

_____   _____

Centre

_____

Instructions to Candidates

1. The time allowed for answering this paper is **two (2) hours.**

2. Fill in your name and the registration number printed on your appointment form in the appropriate spaces on this paper, and on any other sheets that you use.

3. **Do not open this paper until you are told to do so.**

4. This paper contains **seven (7) sections** and you should answer all of them.

5. Read each question carefully before answering it. Your answers must be written legibly in the spaces provided.

6. You are reminded that you are bound by the regulations for written exams displayed at the exam centre and listed on page 4 of the current edition of the written exams syllabus. In particular, you are reminded that you are not allowed to bring books, music or papers into the exam room. Bags must be left at the back of the room under the supervision of the invigilator.

7. If you leave the exam room you will not be allowed to return.

Examiner's use only:

1 (10)	
2 (20)	
3 (10)	
4 (10)	
5 (15)	
6 (15)	
7 (20)	
Total	

Section 1 (10 marks)

Put a tick (✓) in the box next to the correct answer.

Example

Name this note:

A ☐   D ☐   C ☑

This shows that you think **C** is the correct answer.

1.1   Name this note:

C sharp ☐   A sharp ☐   A natural ☐   ☐

1.2   Which is the correct time signature?

$\frac{2}{2}$ ☐ $\frac{3}{2}$ ☐   ¢ ☐   ☐

1.3   For how many crotchet beats does this rest last?

4 ☐   3 ☐   2 ☐   ☐

1.4   Add the total number of crotchet beats in these tied notes:

5 ☐   6 ☐   7 ☐   ☐

1.5   The relative major of E minor is:

G major ☐
F major ☐
C major ☐   ☐

Put a tick (✓) in the box next to the correct answer.

1.6   Which note is the tonic of the minor key shown by this key signature?

E ☐   D ☐   A ☐

1.7   The correct label for the following scale is:

C major scale going up ☐
E harmonic minor scale going up ☐
E natural minor scale going up ☐

1.8   Which chord symbol fits above this tonic triad?

G ☐   Am ☐   Em ☐

1.9   Name this interval:

Major 3rd ☐   Minor 3rd ☐   Major 2nd ☐

1.10   The following is:

E minor tonic triad in root position ☐
C major tonic triad in root position ☐
C major tonic triad in first inversion ☐

(Please turn over for section 2)

3

Section 2 (20 marks)

Boxes for examiner use only

2.1   Write a one-octave A harmonic minor scale in minims, going up.

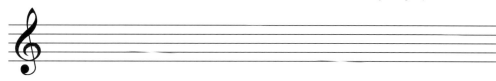

2.2   Using crotchets, write a one-octave arpeggio of F major, going up then down.
       Use a key signature.

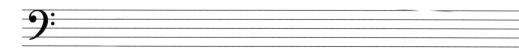

Section 3 (10 marks)

3.1   Circle five different mistakes in the following music, then write it out correctly.

Boxes for
examiner's
use only

Section 4 (10 marks)

4.1 Here is a section of a tune. Make a sequence by repeating it twice, beginning one note higher each time.

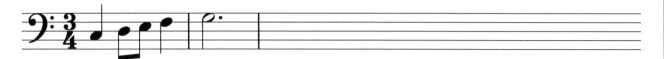

Section 5 (15 marks)

5.1 Transpose this tune up an octave to make it suitable for a tenor voice to sing.

Section 6 (15 marks)

6.1 Write a tune using the first five degrees of the scale of D minor, in any register, to the given rhythm. Use a key signature and finish on the tonic.

Please turn over for Section 7

5

Section 7 (20 marks)

Look at the following piece and answer the questions below and opposite.

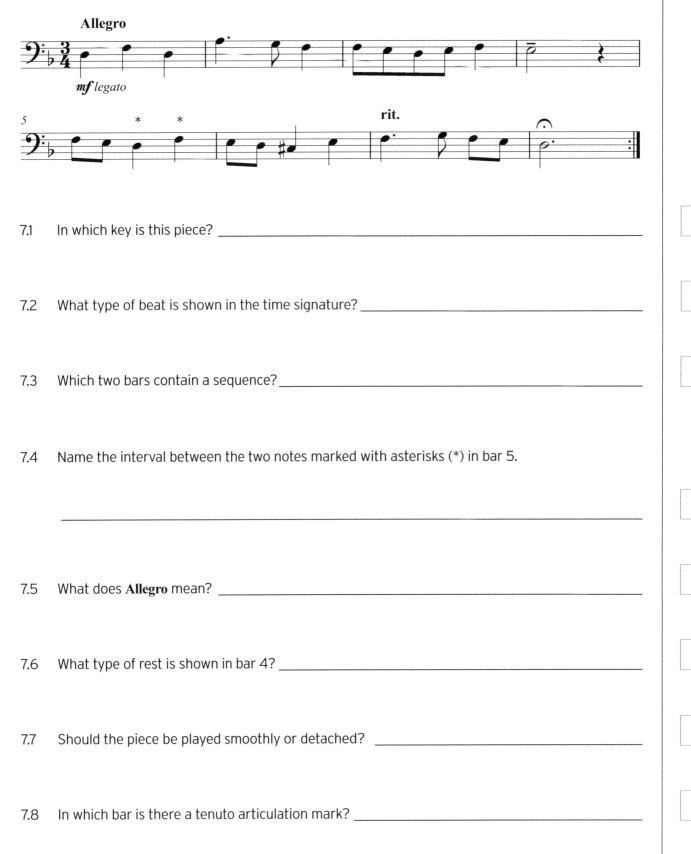

7.1   In which key is this piece? _____

7.2   What type of beat is shown in the time signature? _____

7.3   Which two bars contain a sequence? _____

7.4   Name the interval between the two notes marked with asterisks (*) in bar 5.

        _____

7.5   What does **Allegro** mean? _____

7.6   What type of rest is shown in bar 4? _____

7.7   Should the piece be played smoothly or detached? _____

7.8   In which bar is there a tenuto articulation mark? _____

7.9   In which bar does the music begin to slow down?_____

7.10   Write a Roman numeral below the last note of this piece to show that the tonic triad should
       accompany it.

Theory of Music Grade 2
November 2018

TRINITY
COLLEGE LONDON

Your full name (as on appointment form). Please use BLOCK CAPITALS.

_____

Your signature   Registration number

_____   _____

Centre

_____

Instructions to Candidates

1. The time allowed for answering this paper is **two (2) hours.**

2. Fill in your name and the registration number printed on your appointment form in the appropriate spaces on this paper, and on any other sheets that you use.

3. **Do not open this paper until you are told to do so.**

4. This paper contains **seven (7) sections** and you should answer all of them.

5. Read each question carefully before answering it. Your answers must be written legibly in the spaces provided.

6. You are reminded that you are bound by the regulations for written exams displayed at the exam centre and listed on page 4 of the current edition of the written exams syllabus. In particular, you are reminded that you are not allowed to bring books, music or papers into the exam room. Bags must be left at the back of the room under the supervision of the invigilator.

7. If you leave the exam room you will not be allowed to return.

(D-02)

Section 1 (10 marks)

Boxes for examiner use only

Put a tick (✓) in the box next to the correct answer.

Example

Name this note:

A ☐   D ☐   C ☑

This shows that you think **C** is the correct answer.

1.1   Name this note:

C sharp ☐   D sharp ☐   D natural ☐

☐

1.2   What does the 2 mean in this time signature?

count in crotchet beats ☐

count 2 beats in a bar ☐

count in minim beats ☐

☐

1.3   Which rest(s) fit below the asterisk (*)?

𝄾 𝄾 ☐   𝄽 ☐   𝄾 𝄾 ☐

☐

1.4   Add the total number of quaver beats in these tied notes:

7 ☐   6 ☐   8 ☐

☐

1.5   The relative minor of F major is:

F minor ☐

A minor ☐

D minor ☐

☐

2

Put a tick (✓) in the box next to the correct answer.

1.6 Which note is the tonic of the minor key shown by this key signature?

E ☐   D ☐   A ☐   ☐

1.7 Here is the scale of A natural minor going up. Which degree of the scale will you change to make the scale of A harmonic minor?

1   2   3   4   5   6   7   8(1)

the third degree ☐
the sixth degree ☐
the seventh degree ☐

☐

1.8 Which chord symbol fits above this tonic triad?

C ☐   Am ☐   A ☐   ☐

1.9 Name this interval:

Minor 3rd ☐   Major 3rd ☐   Major 2nd ☐   ☐

1.10 The following is:

G major tonic triad in root position ☐
G major tonic triad in first inversion ☐
E minor tonic triad in first inversion ☐

☐

(Please turn over for section 2)

Section 2 (20 marks)

2.1 Write a one-octave D harmonic minor scale in minims, going up. Do not use a key signature, but add any necessary accidentals.

2.2 Using crotchets, write a one-octave arpeggio of G major, going up then down. Use a key signature.

Section 3 (10 marks)

3.1 Circle five different mistakes in the following music, then write it out correctly.

Section 4 (10 marks)

Boxes for examiner's use only

4.1 Here is a section of a tune. Make a sequence by repeating it twice, beginning one note higher each time.

Section 5 (15 marks)

5.1 Transpose this tune up an octave to make it suitable for a soprano voice to sing.

Section 6 (15 marks)

6.1 Write a tune using the first five degrees of the scale of E minor, in any register, to the given rhythm. Use a key signature and finish on the tonic.

Please turn over for Section 7

5

Section 7 (20 marks)

Look at the following piece and answer the questions below.

7.1 In which key is this piece? _____

7.2 How many phrases are in this piece? _____

7.3 Which phrase contains a sequence? _____

7.4 Name the interval between the two notes marked with asterisks (*) in bar 3.

_____

7.5 What does **Allegretto** mean? _____

7.6 Name the articulation mark above the note in bar 4 and describe how to play it.

_____

7.7 What is the softest dynamic in this piece? _____

7.8 What type of rest is used in bar 8? _____

7.9 Name the note with an accidental in bar 2. _____

7.10 Write a chord symbol above the last note of this piece to show that the tonic triad should accompany it.

THEORY OF MUSIC PAST PAPERS – NOVEMBER 2018 GRADE 2

for Trinity College London written exams

This booklet contains two past exam papers for Trinity College London's Grade 2 exam in music theory, taken from the November 2018 exam sessions. There is no difference in difficulty between the C and D papers.

This booklet can be used in conjunction with the corresponding model answers, which are available to download from **trinitycollege.com/pastpapers**, where you will also find past papers and model answers from other exam sessions.

The Theory of Music Workbook series contains all the requirements of the graded exams and provides step-by-step instructions, suitable for use in lessons or for private study.

Theory of Music Workbook Grade 2   TG 006516   ISBN 978-0-85736-001-4
Theory of Music Workbook Grade 3   TG 006523   ISBN 978-0-85736-002-1

Also available from **trinitycollege.com/shop** or your local music shop:

Handbook of Musical Knowledge   TCL 001191   ISBN 978-0-85736-015-1

All syllabuses and further information about Trinity College London exams can be obtained from **trinitycollege.com**

Copyright © 2019 Trinity College London Press Ltd

TCL 018724
ISBN 978-0-85736-787-7

9 780857 367877